75th
RANGERS

RUSS and SUSAN BRYANT

ZENITH PRESS

First published in 2005 by Zenith Press, an imprint of MBI Publishing Company, Galtier Plaza, Suite 200, 380 Jackson Street, St. Paul, MN 55101-3885 USA

Zenith Press titles are also available at discounts in bulk quantity for industrial or sales-promotional use. For details write to Special Sales Manager at MBI Publishing Company, Galtier Plaza, Suite 200, 380 Jackson Street, St. Paul, MN 55101-3885 USA.

Library of Congress Cataloging-in-Publication Data

Bryant, Russ, 1966
    75th Rangers / by Russ Bryant.
        p. cm. -- (Power Series)
    ISBN 0-7603-2111-6 (PLC)
    1. United States. Army. Ranger Regiment, 75th--History.
    2. United States. Army--Commando troops--History.
    I. Title. II. Power Series (Osceola, Wis.)

UA34.R36B775 2005
356'.1673'0973--dc22

Editors: Steve Gansen and Lindsay Hitch
Designer: Brenda C. Canales

Printed in China

On the front cover: The M24 sniper weapon system uses a Remington 700 bolt-action rifle with a Leopold Mark IV 10-power scope. Snipers are well trained in stalking, concealment, and other movement techniques. Some snipers will avoid certain foods to prevent emitting a detectable odor. They are masters at moving silently without detection.

On the frontispiece: A Ranger takes advantage of all training and schooling opportunities. The combat infantryman's badge (CIB) above the jumpmaster wings is worn proudly on the standard battle dress uniform. This Ranger has also graduated from high-altitude, low-opening (HALO) school, represented by the badge under the U.S. Army name tape.

On the title page: With Task Force 160 special operations aviation wing, Rangers fast rope from a UH-60 direct-action penetrator (DAP) Black Hawk with covering fire provided by 30mm miniguns.

On the back cover: *(top)* The Ranger jumping into the water has 550 cord tied from his poncho-wrapped rucksack to his body so the rucksack won't be separated from him. *(below)* The ranger training department based at Fort Benning, Georgia, is responsible for the demonstrations that the civilians view at ranger school graduations. Graduation is held at Victory Pond, the same place where ranger school begins. Demonstrators show the basics to the observers so they can see some of the training situations the students go though during ranger school.

The ranger training department based at Fort Benning, Georgia, is responsible for the demonstrations that the civilians view at ranger school graduations. Observers can see some of the training situations that students go through during ranger school.

About the authors: Russ Bryant is a veteran of 1st Ranger Battalion from 1985 to 1989. Following his service, Russ attended Savannah College of Art and Design and received a Bachelors of Fine Art Degree in Photography. As a photographer and Ranger veteran, his passions quite naturally led him to photograph Rangers in the tactical environment. He has photographed the 75th Ranger Regiment extensively over the last several years, including the 1st Ranger Battalion at Hunter Army Air Field, the 3rd Ranger Battalion at Fort Benning, and the 2nd Ranger Battalion at Fort Lewis, Washington. Ranger Bryant also had the opportunity to deploy with 3rd Ranger Battalion to Germany.

Susan Bryant has followed the 75th Ranger Regiment since the mid-1980s and became associated with the special operations forces community when she married then-U.S. Army Ranger Russ Bryant. Since that time, she has lived in Germany and Savannah, Georgia. Her experience with and knowledge of the local military community is extensive. She was a significant researcher and contributor for photographer Russ Bryant's *To Be a U.S. Army Ranger* (MBI Publishing, 2003). Susan holds a bachelor's degree from Furman University, and Master of Education and Education Specialist degrees from Georgia Southern University. Initially a special education teacher, she now spends her days as a public school psychologist and a writer for Savannah's monthly magazine, *Island Living*. During her leisure time, she enjoys reading, traveling, and relaxing in her hammock.

Contents

Acknowledgments

I would like to thank the men of the 75th Ranger Regiment for the continued support and access they've given to help me complete this book. I also thank the U.S. Army Special Operations Command Public Affairs Office staff, Carol Darby and Barbara Ashley. I appreciate the support of the Army Public Affairs Office in New York City, Captain Kevin Matthews, S-5 of the 1st Ranger Battalion; Sergeant First Class Chris Gerigen of Headquarters and Headquarters Company (HHC),1st Ranger Battalion; and Sergeant Odie Morehouse from the 1st Ranger Battalion. I deeply appreciate Steve Gansen at MBI Publishing Company for his friendship and guidance on another great book project. A special thanks goes to my wife, Susan, for writing a wonderful book and for supplying her constant support and dedication to my mission. I owe gratitude to my friends and family for their understanding and support while I've worked on this book over the past months, especially Morgan and Travis, my children.

—Russ Bryant, photographer

Introduction

The advent of the Ranger came in seventeenth-century North America, where English settlements had to learn how to defend themselves against Native American attacks. The colonists first established mini-forts at major avenues of approach to their settlements, but the sly Indians stealthily slipped past the forts, raided the settlements, and withdrew before the local settlers could organize their militia to fend off the attack and mount a counterattack. In order to survive, the colonists needed an equally secretive force that would learn from and utilize the Indians' own techniques.

By the mid- to late 1630s, Virginia and Maryland plantation owners began to hire small private parties, or Rangers, to discreetly patrol the perimeters of their plantations and give warning of approaching Indians. Maryland employed Rangers to patrol its frontier by 1648, Virginia regularly employed Rangers from 1676, and the practice continued in both colonies into the early eighteenth century. Northern colonies, such as Nova Scotia, New York, Plymouth, and Massachusetts, followed suit and employed Rangers to protect their frontiers during much of the eighteenth century.

The earliest organized ranger unit using ranger-type tactics was activated in 1670 to combat a hostile Wampanoag tribe under the leadership of Chief Metacomet, also called King Philip, in southeastern Massachusetts. The Wampanoag Indians comfortably navigated the harsh lands by foot over great distances. They employed concealment; long-range scouting; and swift, savage raids against their opponents, inflicting a devastating toll on colonists and their property. Standard European tactics were no match for this combination of rugged terrain and skilled enemy. Small groups of Captain Benjamin Church's men sent scouts from the settlements and into the surrounding territory to observe signs of the enemy and provide early warning of approaching Indian raiding parties. Accounts from these scout groups include words such as, "This day, ranged 9 miles." Thus, the term "Ranger" was born. Under the command of Captain Church, the Rangers adopted the Indian's tactics by using reconnaissance procedures and moving swiftly on foot or horseback to raid the Indian positions. They were successful from the start and expanded their over-land raids to the water as well. The Rangers crushed the Indian attacks, ended King Philip's War in 1675, and ended King Philip's life in 1676.

The first ranger company was founded March 23, 1756, as the British Army's Ranger Company of the New Hampshire Provincial Regiment. This unit's name was changed to His Majesty's Independent Company of American Rangers, commonly known as Robert Rogers' Rangers. This ranger company was comprised of 50 privates, three sergeants, one ensign, one lieutenant, and one captain, all paid and employed by the British Army.

During the French and Indian War (1754–1763), soldier Robert Rogers developed the warrior concept to an extent never known before. Operating in the days when commanders personally recruited their men, he was articulate and persuasive, and knew his trade. Rogers had a magnetic personality and raised nine additional companies of American colonists to fight for the British during the French and Indian War. Their intent was to distress and destroy the enemy wherever and whenever possible. Reconnaissance and scouting, ambushes and raids, and prisoner snatches were the primary missions of the colonial-era Rangers. Rogers carried out missions with small ranger patrols that, when they encountered a large and powerful force, would disperse and rally at another location.

Rogers' rate of success was undeniable. His most notorious expedition was an exceptional deep raid against the Abenaki Indians, a fierce and violent force. In October 1759, with 200 Rangers moving by boat and traversing the land, Rogers covered 400 miles in about 60 days. Losses were encountered en route, but the Rangers successfully penetrated deep into Indian territory. The Rangers stealthily raided and destroyed the settlement, killing several hundred enemies, thus extinguishing the threat of the Abenaki Indians. Even more important, this deep raid movement demonstrated that it was possible for the Rangers to strike an enemy force previously perceived as out of reach. Rogers' implementation of the deep raid—striking the enemy within its own area of operation—has become the Rangers' tactical trademark.

Over the next 50 years, every conflict included American frontiersmen formed into ranger companies and led by exceptional commanders in land and water movements, ambushes and raids, and reconnaissance patrols. On June 14, 1775, with war against the British looming dangerously close, the Continental Congress declared that six companies of expert riflemen immediately be formed. In 1777, George Washington called this force of frontiersmen "The Corps of Rangers." Under the leadership of Colonel Daniel Morgan, these ranger companies from Pennsylvania, Virginia, and Maryland earned a reputation as the most famous corps of the Continental Army. They were not Rangers in the strictest sense, but were superior marksmen and, according to one British general, a corps of crack shots. Morgan's Riflemen achieved an impressive victory against the British at the battle of Cowpens in 1781. Attacked by 1,100 British soldiers, Morgan's Rangers killed 110 and captured 830, with a loss of 12 soldiers killed and 63 wounded.

Morgan's Rangers was not the only successful ranger outfit of the Revolutionary War. Thomas Knowlton, a gallant and brave officer according to General George Washington, led the ranger unit from Connecticut. Comprised of less than 150 men, their missions were primarily reconnaissance, to gain vital information for the revolutionists' cause. Patriot Nathan Hale was a captain in Knowlton's unit of Connecticut Rangers. Hale willingly volunteered for the reconnaissance mission on Long Island, New York, that resulted in his execution as a spy by the British on September 22, 1776. At 21 years old, he was hanged from an apple tree in Rutgers' orchard by order of General William Howe without a trial and without granting his request for a Bible.

In the southern region during the Revolutionary War, a ranger element was organized by the infamous Francis Marion. Operating out of the South Carolina swamps along low-lying riverbeds, Marion's men, numbering several hundred, disrupted British communications and supply trains and captured enemy troops. In most cases, Marion's strategy involved hitting the British hard and fast to rapidly destroy their forces and supplies, and then fade into the dense tupelo and cypress woods and swamps before British

reinforcements could arrive. Marion and his men were chased by English forces several times, but were never caught. British Colonel Banastre Tarleton once pursued Marion's men through swamps for approximately 25 miles. Unsuccessful at attaining his mark, Tarleton halted his exhausted and soggy men and cursed, "The damned fox; the devil himself could not catch him." From that time on, Marion was known as the Swamp Fox. To the scorn and distaste of the British, tactics of guerrilla-like warfare were successfully used even in areas allegedly conquered and controlled by British forces.

During the War of 1812, Congress called for the formation of new ranger units to serve on the Western frontier and protect border towns against attacks by American Indians. The December 28, 1813, issue of the Army Register lists officers for 12 companies of Rangers. In the 1830s, the Texas Rangers were established along the Texas border, and their primary mission was to defend settlements from attacking Indians and enforce laws for unruly Texans. During that time, the U.S. Army maintained a 600-man battalion of horseback-mounted Rangers on the vast Western frontier. During the war with Mexico (1846–1848), some Texas Rangers served under the direction of the U.S. Army. Other than these accounts, there were very few official ranger units until the Civil War.

At the time of the Civil War, many confederate ranger units were formed, although very few operated as true ranger units and instead simply took the ranger name, wreaking havoc on whoever crossed their path. By February 1864, few ranger units were left in the Confederate Army, but those few were expertly effective. Perhaps the best-known Rangers of the Civil War period were commanded by Confederate Colonel John S. Mosby. Beginning as a three-man scout unit in 1862, Mosby's force grew into eight companies of Rangers by 1865. Mosby deployed small numbers on his raids, usually 20 to 50 men, and they successfully infiltrated and operated behind Union lines. Greatly influenced by Swamp Fox Francis Marion, Mosby's Rangers used aggressive action and surprise assaults to confuse enemies and diffuse their strength. Scouts conducted reconnaissance and located weak links in their opponents' defense, then they attacked and acquired victory.

The Rangers under the command of Colonel Turner Ashby were equally skilled. Ashby's Rangers served the Confederacy well as they scouted and raided large numbers of Union troops. Confederate General John Hunt Morgan and his cavalry unit formed in December 1861 and moved deep into Union territory, causing widespread hysteria and diverting federal soldiers from the approaching Battle of Chickamauga. General Morgan and his Rangers were finally forced to surrender near East Liverpool, Ohio.

Ranger units were part of Union troop forces as well. Captain Samuel C. Means' Rangers succeeded in engaging and capturing a portion of Colonel Mosby's force, but they never quite accomplished their original mission of eliminating Mosby's Rangers. Means' Rangers did their fair share of capturing troops and seizing supply trains, raiding homesteads and cities, and disturbing communication routes. After the close of the Civil War, recognized army ranger units would disappear for more than 70 years.

Chapter 1

TO THE REGIMENT

Family members of Rangers from 1st Battalion stationed at Hunter Army Airfield in Savannah, Georgia, greet them on the runway of the airfield. The men of 1st Battalion have just returned from combat patrols and operations in northeastern Afghanistan and Operation Anaconda.

The official name "Ranger" was selected by Major General Lucian K. Truscott, United States liaison with the British general staff during World War II. Truscott submitted proposals to U.S. Army Chief of Staff General George Marshall that they "undertake immediately an American unit along the lines of the British Commandos." Truscott reasoned that the "name 'commandos' rightfully belonged to the British, and we sought a name more typically American." Furthermore, the name "Ranger" held an honored place in American history, after the esteemed eighteenth- and nineteenth-century Rangers of the French and Indian War, the Revolutionary War, and the Civil War. Rangers had adopted the British Commandos' standards and techniques in colonial America more than 200 years before. In the twentieth century,

British commandos demonstrated success with special operations techniques in the European theater, and General Marshall recognized the need to coordinate training between U.S. and British troops. Eventually, six ranger battalions were activated during World War II.

On June 19, 1942, the 1st Ranger Battalion was activated in Carrickfergus, Ireland. The battalion was formed by volunteers drawn from regular U.S. Army units based in Northern Ireland. Then-Major William Orlando Darby was appointed as the battalion's first commander. He organized, trained, and led carefully selected men to conduct key World War II missions in North Africa, Tunisia, and Italy, to name a few. His record of success astounded military leaders, who bestowed upon him the task of organizing two additional ranger battalions, the 3rd and

Phil Piazza of South Carolina attends a ranger school graduation at Fort Benning, Georgia. Mr. Piazza was a lieutenant and weapons platoon leader in Burma fighting with the legendary Merrill's Marauders, who saw fierce combat with the Chinese. A significant number of Marauders fell ill to diseases and snakebites.

A Ranger from the 1st Ranger Battalion, 75th Ranger Regiment, receives the Silver Star of valor against an armed enemy while conducting combat operations in the mountains of Afghanistan.

At a family day celebration, a television news woman innocently asks a Ranger's young son, "Honey, what does your daddy do in the army?" Without hesitation, the boy flatly answers, "He clears rooms."

At Fort Benning, Georgia, near Building 4, the Ranger Memorial has bricks representing past and present Rangers. No rank is used in the title on the brick, just the word "Ranger."

4th. His active participation in these units led to the 1st, 3rd, and 4th Ranger Battalions, to be known as Darby's Rangers.

The 2nd Ranger Battalion, activated on April 1, 1943, was trained and led by Lieutenant Colonel James Earl Rudder, who successfully carried out the most dangerous mission of the Omaha Beach landings in Normandy, France. On June 6, 1944, three companies of the 2nd Ranger Battalion scaled the 100-foot perpendicular cliffs leading to Point Du Hoc with rope ladders and grapples under intense gunfire. Upon reaching the point, they assaulted the imbedded German positions and destroyed a large gun battery that would have wreaked havoc on the Allied fleets offshore. For two days and nights they fought without relief.

During the initial assault on Omaha Beach, Brigadier General Norman D. Cota, assistant division commander of the 29th Infantry Division, realized that the invasion force must push on past the beach or suffer intolerable losses. Brigadier General Cota chose the 5th Ranger Battalion, led by Lieutenant Colonel Max Schneider, to make a way through the murderous German artillery fire. Although his exact words may be debated, Brigadier General Cota clearly communicated the expectation and confidence that the Rangers would lead the way off Omaha Beach and to the seawall. Brigadier General Cota's statement has become the familiar motto, "Rangers lead the way."

Though not called Rangers, the servicemen in the 5307th Composite Unit (Provisional) carried out ranger-type missions in northern Burma from February to August 1944. The unit's commander, Major General Frank D. Merrill, fearlessly and valiantly led the 5307th, and the unit became known

Rangers from A company, 1st Ranger Battalion, stand silently and at attention in desert battle dress uniforms (BDUs) under the American flag. They have just returned from a combat deployment in Afghanistan, and other members of the battalion and family members greet them at Hunter Army Airfield in Savannah, Georgia.

as Merrill's Marauders for their stamina, perseverance, and professionalism. During a campaign in Southeast Asia in 1944, Major General Merrill and his Marauders distinguished themselves by climbing mountains, crossing rivers, and maneuvering through jungles to surprise the enemy. These men fought sickness and exhaustion, and the Japanese. The group was disbanded after three months of fighting, during which 80 percent of its 3,000 volunteers were lost to disease and combat. Merrill's Marauders concluded their missions with the

successful seizure of Myitkyina Airfield in north Burma. By the standards of today's veteran groups, Merrill's Marauders are considered Rangers.

The 6th Ranger Battalion, commanded by Lieutenant Colonel Henry Mace, was formed in September 1944 in the Pacific Theater and was the only ranger unit specifically organized and trained to conduct special operations missions during World War II. Operations were conducted by task force-, platoon-, or company-sized elements. All of the 6th Ranger

The eye of the sniper is one of his most important assets. Snipers work in pairs, with a spotter and shooter. The more experienced senior ranking man is the spotter. The spotter marks targets and assesses wind direction and distance.

Battalion's missions were behind enemy lines and involved long-range reconnaissance and combat patrols. Their objectives—conducted and successfully completed during a fierce Pacific storm—included destroying coastal defense guns, radio stations, and other means of communications on three islands in Leyte Bay. In January 1945, the 6th Ranger Battalion conducted a daring mission to rescue American and Allied prisoners of war in the Philippines. The Rangers made a 29-mile forced march past enemy lines in search of the Japanese prison camp at Cabanatuan, Philippines. They located the camp; crawled almost a mile over flat, exposed terrain; attacked Japanese positions; and rescued more than 500 prisoners of war.

The ranger units were deactivated in 1945, disbanded just as they had been after each of America's previous conflicts. In 1950, the army chief of staff selected Colonel John Gibson Van Houton to create a ranger training program at Fort Benning, Georgia. These trainees were regular army volunteers, and many were from the 82nd Airborne Division. Some of the ranger training volunteers had fought with the ranger battalions during World War II. Many of the training instructors were drawn from this same group of World War II–era Rangers. Training began in October 1950, with three companies of airborne-qualified personnel who completed their training on November 13, 1950.

Once reactivated and trained, Rangers again distinguished themselves in combat during the Korean War (1950–1953).

Ranger instructors demonstrate hand-to-hand fighting techniques for families and visitors at a ranger school graduation at Fort Benning. The instructors put on a good show, demonstrating several types of hand-to-hand and knife-fighting skills.

A new Ranger in the 1st Ranger Battalion reports to the expert infantryman's badge (EIB) test site hand-grenade station without his modular information communications helmet (MICH). The grader quickly supplies the Ranger with a helmet, since safety is a must. Many Rangers excel at throwing hand grenades due to their athletic prowess and the military's high standards of physical fitness.

A C-17 drops Rangers on a small airfield in South Carolina to start instruction on ranger equipment and weapons for other military units. Rangers jump from C-130, C-141, and C-17 aircraft.

The graduates of the ranger training program were organized into eight companies, each of which was attached to a conventional infantry division, including the 2nd Infantry

Division, 3rd Infantry Division, 7th Infantry Division, 24th Infantry Division, 25th Infantry Division, and 1st Cavalry Division. One airborne ranger company of approximately 100 men was attached to each infantry division numbering 18,000 men. Somewhat nomadic, the ranger units were attached first to one regiment in the division and then to another regiment. From December 1950 through the spring of 1951, the Korean-era Rangers performed scouting, patrols, raids, ambushes,

The C-17 provides a great jumping platform for the Rangers. The C-17 holds a massive amount of cargo and has room for 50 Rangers fully rigged with combat equipment and two desert mobility vehicles (DMVs).

On January 15, 2004, at Hunter Army Airfield, Rangers from the 1st Ranger Battalion receive Bronze Stars and Army Commendation Medals for their actions in Iraq and Afghanistan.

On the Darby Queen obstacle course at Fort Benning, home of the 3rd Ranger Battalion, Rangers ascend a rope net ladder at the end of the grueling course. The Rangers have only a 150-yard sprint over hilly terrain to complete the course. Rangers complete the course in buddy teams, which requires both men to reach the end.

assaults, and counterattacked forces to restore lost positions. The Rangers provided American forces with sterling performance by catching the opposition unaware with nighttime operations, infiltrating enemy strongholds by surprise, executing raids deep behind enemy lines, and navigating the land with unprecedented success. Consistent with prior practice, the Rangers were again deactivated at the end of the Korean conflict in 1951 and reassigned to other units.

Soon after U.S. Army commanders arrived in Vietnam, they realized the pressing need for an elite reconnaissance element that could conduct long-range surveillance on an elusive enemy and provide the combat intelligence required to accomplish needed missions. Through a complex reorganization maneuver, the small long-range reconnaissance patrol (LRRP) units inherited the proud ranger lineage, and these forces were eventually designated as the 75th Infantry Regiment

Previous Page: Colonel Ralph Puckett (Ret.), the honorary colonel of the 75th Ranger Regiment, congratulates ranger school students. Ranger school gives the Ralph Puckett Award to an officer who meets graduation criteria by passing all graded leadership positions, passing all peer reports, losing no major equipment, having all spot reports cancelled, receiving no recycles (other than medical), and requiring no re-tests on critical tasks.

On the ramp of a C-130, Rangers from the Regimental Reconnaissance Detachment (Team 3) conduct high-altitude, low-opening (HALO) operations. The teams are the eyes and ears of each battalion's headquarters elements. These highly schooled senior noncommissioned officers (NCOs) report enemy activity and strength prior to the main body of Rangers' assault on their objective. Under most conditions, the men in each team have served in the battalion for which they are conducting reconnaissance.

All regimental reconnaissance detachment (RRD) teams are high-altitude, low-opening (HALO) and scuba qualified, and usually have an E-6 or higher rank. The RRD teams' main missions are to report enemy activity to the chain of command and verify targets that will be hit by Rangers at a later time.

(Ranger) in 1969. The LRRP units performed many jobs similar to that of Rangers. Thirteen of the fifteen ranger companies were assigned to brigades, divisions, and field units to act as eyes and ears in the land claimed by the Viet Cong and the North Vietnamese Army.

Like their predecessors, Vietnam-era Rangers were very effective in their jobs. They worked in six-man teams, carried everything needed on their backs, and lived off the land by eating rice and other local foods. The Rangers attacked the enemy using hit-and-run raids and ambushes. From the Mekong Delta to the demilitarized zone in Vietnam, Rangers exploited enemy operations in denied-access areas and provided invaluable combat intelligence. A group of U.S. Rangers was assigned as training team advisors for the Army of the Republic of Vietnam Rangers (Biêt Dông Quân or BDQ), which was initially organized into companies to counter guerrilla warfare being waged by the Viet Cong.

At the close of the Vietnam War, the ranger companies were deactivated, and the men were dispersed among the various army units, with most being reassigned to the 82nd Airborne Division at Fort Bragg, North Carolina. The Rangers proudly served with distinction until their unit's deactivation on August 15, 1972.

Chapter 2

ORIGINS

The ranger battalion is to be an elite, light, and most proficient infantry battalion in the world; a battalion that can do things with its hands and weapons better than anyone. The battalion will not contain any "hoodlums" or "brigands," and if the battalion is formed of such persons, it will be disbanded. Wherever the battalion goes, it will be apparent that it is the best.

Abrams Charter, General Creighton Abrams, army chief of staff, 1973

Any Ranger who maintains the high standards of the ranger battalion has the opportunity to attend special schools that teach additional techniques and procedures related to their military occupational specialty. Some of the more common schools are jumpmaster school, high-altitude, low-opening (HALO), and pathfinder school.

The Birth of the Regiment

In the days of the Holy Roman Empire, soldiers bore a shield and carried a sword or spear. As our nation laid its foundation, Revolutionary and Civil War soldiers armed themselves with a hatchet and a rifle, and possibly a few dozen rounds of ammunition. They traveled light with only a canteen, a wool blanket, and minimal food provisions. The modern light infantryman's load is nothing but light in comparison to his predecessors. Armed with a fully automatic rifle, hundreds of rounds of ammunition, various grenades, night-vision optics, and radio communications, the infantry soldier is ready for whatever he encounters. His load increases as he dons protective body armor; a helmet; and water, food, and medical supplies.

During operations in the eighteenth and nineteenth centuries, early predecessors to today's Rangers used the best available means of transportation. If circumstances permitted, they rode horseback, but horses were only used for transportation, with fighting done on foot for greater stealth and maneuverability. Using boats whenever possible, early Rangers conducted waterborne patrols and amphibious raids as early as the late seventeenth century. Units in New England sometimes conducted their winter ranging operations on snowshoes and ice skates. From the seventeenth through the late nineteenth century, Rangers provided their own weapons, clothing, equipment, and horses. In return, they were paid higher wages than other soldiers. For example, a U.S. Ranger (1812–1815) received one dollar per day—three times the normal army serviceman's pay. Rangers seldom wore standard uniforms, although they did manage to standardize their weapons and equipment within companies, and their firearms were normally the very best they could find.

The 75th Ranger Regiment is a flexible, highly trained, and rapidly deployable light-infantry force with specialized skills that enable it to be

Carrying his M4 with an Aimpoint red dot scope and PAQ-laser target designator, this young Ranger has already experienced combat in the Middle East several times. The regiment has new Rhodesian assault vests and equipment that offer increased comfort and greater freedom of movement in the lower body.

A UH-60 Black Hawk helicopter hovers in place to drop Rangers in Victory Pond at Fort Benning. The Rangers jump together so they can stay close and recover their equipment and weapons, which are tied by 550 cord to each jumper.

employed against a variety of conventional and special operations targets. The mission of the 75th Ranger Regiment is direct action (DA): to plan and conduct special military operations in any operational environment. These Rangers are the nation's premier strike force capable of conducting small-unit operations any time and any place. Rangers are ready to deploy anywhere in the world with only an 18-hour notice. They are experts at infiltrating by land, sea, or air, into any kind of terrain, and under any type of condition.

Give a Ranger a mission and it will be done right the first time and in a well-planned, well-rehearsed manner. He may arrive by parachuting from an airplane, fast roping from a hovering helicopter, or jumping out the back of a transport. In some cases, the helicopter may even hover long enough for the Ranger to step off directly to the ground, but then he will be off and running. If the terrain prohibits running, the Ranger will swim, climb, crawl, rappel, hop, skip, or jump with speed. He will cross rivers, move through jungles, scale mountain cliffs, and

assault beachfronts. This elite warrior will not be alone. His comrades will be there beside him, operating with the same expertise, intensity, and motivation. Together and individually, they will uphold the tenets of the Ranger Creed.

Prompted by the 1973 Arab-Israeli Conflict, the U.S. Department of the Army recognized the need for a light, specialized mobile force that could move quickly to any trouble spot in the world. In the fall of 1973, General Creighton Abrams, army chief of staff, formulated the idea of reforming a ranger force. General Abrams declared that the organization of the ranger battalion must be done right, with careful prioritization of strategic goals and allocation of equipment and facilities.

On January 25, 1974, activation of the 1st Battalion, 75th Infantry (Ranger), was authorized with an effective date of January 31, 1974. This was the first battalion-sized ranger unit since World War II, and General Abrams personally selected the first officers. He believed that a tough, disciplined, and elite

During a break at the best ranger competition, conducted at Fort Benning, Georgia, a member from the 1st Ranger Battalion takes time to mentally prepare for the next event.

Members of 3rd Ranger Battalion conduct a live-fire exercise and rush to clear buildings and trenches around the objective. These Rangers are bounding up under the support element's fire dug in the distant wood line.

ranger unit would set a standard for the U.S. Army. In these early days, Rangers were often referred to as "Abrams' Own."

In February 1974, selection began and personnel assembled at Fort Benning, Georgia, to undergo training from March through June 1974. On July 1, 1974, the 1st Battalion, 75th Infantry (Ranger), parachuted into Fort Stewart, Georgia, marking the unit's activation.

On October 1, 1974, the 2nd Battalion, 75th Ranger Regiment, was activated at Fort Lewis, Washington. This battalion traces its lineage back to Merrill's Marauders of Burma in World War II.

Present-day ranger battalions were first called upon in April 1980. Elements of the 1st Battalion, 75th Infantry (Ranger), participated in the Desert One mission to rescue the American embassy personnel held hostage in Teheran, Iran. Primarily a special forces operation, the 1st Special Forces Operational Detachment—Delta was to perform the actual hostage rescue. The Rangers knew their mission as Operation Eagle Claw, and

Rangers from the 2nd Ranger Battalion prepare to disembark from an MH-6 Little Bird from Task Force 160, formally known as the 160th Special Operations Aviation Regiment (Airborne). The MH-6 Little Bird carries four Rangers to a rooftop to clear the buildings during a training operation at Fort Bragg, North Carolina.

C Company, 1st Battalion, 75th Infantry (Ranger) was tasked with providing security for the special forces men, hostages, and equipment. The Rangers were to fly from Egypt to a city 35 miles south of Teheran and secure the airfield there. Once the airfield was secured, the Rangers would maintain control as C-141s arrived to airlift the hostages and their rescuers back to Egypt. Desert One was aborted at the first stage when two Sea Stallions crashed into each other on landing, killing the crews.

Training and preparation for Operation Eagle Claw established the groundwork for the Rangers and special operations forces. Ranger training continued, as did the army's belief in their capabilities. The training focused on special operations. In 1980, the 2nd Battalion trained throughout the world and participated in combat; shows of force; and demonstrations of duration in key regions of England, Thailand, Central and South America, and Africa.

The proven combat effectiveness of the 1st and 2nd Ranger Battalions during their deployment to Grenada on October 25, 1983, underscored General Abrams' decision to authorize this elite infantry force. As a result of their combat effectiveness in Grenada, the

U.S. Army sniper school produces highly lethal sharpshooters. Camouflage techniques are taught, and snipers design their own Ghillie suits to disguise their presence in a specific environment. Ghillie suits were developed by Scottish game wardens in the eighteenth century to catch poachers.

Department of the Army announced in 1984 that it was increasing the ranger force to its highest level in 40 years by activating another ranger battalion and a ranger regimental headquarters. The Department of the Army activated the 3rd Ranger Battalion on October 3, 1984, and the 75th Ranger Regimental Headquarters on February 3, 1986, both stationed at Fort Benning, Georgia. The ranger force had grown to over 2,000 by 1984.

The 75th Ranger Regiment is the premier light-infantry unit of the United States Army. The 75th Ranger Regiment's mission is to plan and conduct special missions in support of U.S. policy and objectives. The three ranger battalions that comprise the 75th Ranger Regiment are geographically dispersed. Their locations are:
• 1st Battalion, 75th Ranger Regiment, Hunter Army Airfield, Georgia
• 2nd Battalion, 75th Ranger Regiment, Fort Lewis, Washington
• 3rd Battalion, 75th Ranger Regiment, Fort Benning, Georgia

Headquartered at Fort Benning near Columbus, Georgia, A ranger battalion is authorized 580 men with up to 15 percent overstaffing due to TDY and attending schools. According to fiscal year 2001 data, the ranger regiment had an estimated

A Ranger armed with an MK46 5.56mm machine gun with an advanced compact optical gun (ACOG) sight 4x scope engages targets on a stress fire course for the 3rd Ranger Battalion. Rangers run and crawl to the objective, and then must accurately engage targets 50 meters away before moving to the next obstacles and repeating the process. Rangers train in stressful situations to simulate combat operations.

Fast roping is an insertion technique special operations forces use to get on the ground quickly and move to an objective without landing the aircraft. With Task Force 160 special operations aviation wing, Rangers fast rope from a UH-60 direct-action penetrator (DAP) Black Hawk with covering fire provided by 30mm miniguns.

2,300 men, a number that's expected to grow in light of a recent ranger indoctrination program (RIP) class enrolling 575 men, the largest RIP class in ranger history. Each ranger battalion is identical in its organization, with three rifle or combat companies, a battalion headquarters company, and a headquarters company. The battalion headquarters company includes the company's headquarters, the fire-support team, the medical team, and the communications team. There is also a support section that includes food services.

Each of the ranger battalion's rifle companies consists of approximately 150 Rangers each, with the remaining men in the battalion assigned to battalion headquarters or the company's headquarters company. Each rifle company is comprised of a headquarters and headquarters company, three rifle platoons of about 45 men each, and a weapons platoon of 20 or so men. Members of the rifle squads carry a lightweight automatic weapon with them on assaults, and squad medics also carry a rifle.

After commando-crawling across a rope suspended 50 feet above Victory Pond at Fort Benning, a Ranger drops to the water, reciting a stanza of the Ranger Creed.

After hitting the water, he will swim to shore and receive instructions to either do it again or move to the next phase of the water confidence course.

The Ranger Uniform

Rangers of the 75th Ranger Regiment received official authorization through AR 670-5, Uniform and Insignia, January 30, 1975, to wear the black beret with their battle dress uniforms and dress uniforms. Locally authorized black berets had been worn briefly by certain ranger and long-range reconnaissance patrol (LRRP) companies during the Korean and Vietnam Wars. Armor and armored cavalry personnel wore black berets as distinctive headgear until Command Sergeant of the Army (CSA) Bernard W. Rogers banned all unofficial headgear in 1979. In October 2000, Army Chief of Staff General Eric K. Shinseki announced that the black berets distinctive of the 75th Ranger Regiment would be the army's standard headgear effective June 14, 2001. Special operations and airborne soldiers could continue to wear their distinctive berets—soldiers in airborne units wear maroon berets, and special forces soldiers wear green berets. In response to this change in the dress code and desiring to remain visually distinctive from other service member and units, the 75th Ranger Regiment adopted the tan beret with the approval of General Shinseki, effective June 2001.

The black beret distinctively marks the Rangers as an elite and separate unit from others. Ranger soldiers are known the world over as the epitome of the infantryman. A Ranger is a warrior of indomitable will. He is a consummate leader who thrives on adversity and inspires total trust and confidence in his ability to do what is right in any situation. A Ranger is a uniquely qualified soldier who will fight and win anywhere in the world. As history has proven, whenever the United States is involved in a conflict, a ranger force has been and will be involved.

A definitive day in Ranger history, the ranger regiment was required to surrender the coveted black beret and replace it with the tan beret. In ceremony, Army Chief of Staff General Eric Shinseki has the Rangers parade off the field in the new tan beret that will become the symbol of a new chapter in ranger history. After the Rangers gave up the black beret, the army adopted the distinctive head gear as its own and the regular U.S. Army service members wear it to this day.

Red-hot metal glows from a Browning M2 .50-caliber heavy machine gun on the support berm. An MH-53 drags the 50 on a Skedko, a stretcher also used to take the wounded and those killed in action (KIA) off the battlefield. Once the weapon is put into a covering fire position, it will greatly increase the firepower of the support and assault elements attacking the objective.

The weapons platoon contains three sections: a mortar section, an antitank section, and a sniper section. The mortar section has two 60mm mortars, with a third available for special operations when needed. The antitank section is supplied with three three-man teams for the 84mm Carl Gustav recoilless rifle. The weapons platoon also encompasses the highly and specifically trained ranger sniper team. These two-man teams can engage targets at 1,000 meters with deadly accuracy. The weapons platoon also has two two-man sniper teams armed with the M24 and a third two-man team armed with the .50-caliber Barrett sniper system.

Each ranger battalion has a ranger support element that operates in support of the ranger's training at their home station.

This unit of parachute riggers, truck drivers, maintenance workers, and the like provides the battalion with all the necessary services to meet training, mission, and deployment demands. It is important to note that the ranger support element, although responsible for supporting the ranger force's outload for combat, does not deploy with the ranger battalion. The logistical and support arrangements for extended missions in a deployed environment remain a constant ranger concern.

The Making of a Ranger

All officers and enlisted soldiers in the regiment are four-time volunteers—for the army, the airborne school, the ranger regiment, and the ranger school. Volunteers selected for the 75th

Weighted down with gear, supplies, weaponry, and ammunition, a Ranger takes a load off his feet when the time is appropriate and available. Although he is sitting, he is always alert to his surroundings and ready to move out to the next objective. Squads and platoons rotate missions and responsibilities to provide the men with equal opportunity for rest, meals, and priorities of work, such as personal hygiene and weapon maintenance.

A ranger school student moves slowly through the humid, soggy swamps on patrol. His squad is ready for possible enemy contact. The students are in the final phase of the army's most demanding school—the ranger course. This school teaches combat leadership skills that will stay with its graduates throughout their military careers and life.

The point man leads the way in the swamps of Florida. During the planning phase of an operations order, the patrol leader finds the best man to be on point, someone with excellent land navigation skills. The patrol leader designates the best men to fill all the positions in the squad according to each man's strengths and weaknesses.

The mountains of Dahlonega, Georgia, are used in the mountain phase of ranger school, which offers many opportunities to rappel from very high elevations. The Rangers will buddy rappel and night rappel as well.

Ranger Regiment must meet tough physical, mental, and moral criteria. All commissioned officers and combat arms noncommissioned officers (NCOs) must be airborne and ranger qualified, and must exhibit a demonstrated proficiency in the duty position that they are seeking.

The soldier's journey to a ranger battalion begins in basic combat training (BCT). Many refer to this training as simply "basic" or "basic training." All who enlist in the army complete this required eight-week course, which is the basis for all other training that the soldier will receive, no matter which military occupational specialty (MOS) he chooses. This training begins at a primary level and builds over time.

Advanced infantry training (AIT) is the next step for the soldier on his way to one of the three ranger battalions, and is necessary for the soldier to obtain a military occupational specialty (MOS). Upon completion, the infantrymen proceed to the basic airborne course (BAC), also known as jump school. The purpose of the three-week BAC is to qualify the soldier in the use of the parachute as a means of combat deployment and to develop leadership, self-confidence, and an aggressive spirit through mental and physical conditioning.

The new MK46 5.56mm machine gun has a maximum range of 800 meters and a cyclic rate of fire of 650 rounds per minute. Rangers cross-train on all weapons systems so a crew-served weapon system or greater-casualty-producing weapon isn't left without an operator. Any Ranger can take the lead ammunition position and drive on to the mission.

Ranger training began at Fort Benning, Georgia, in September 1950, when the ranger training command formed and trained 17 airborne ranger companies during the Korean War. In October 1951, the U.S. Army Infantry School established the ranger department and extended ranger training to all combat units in the army. On November 1, 1987, the ranger department reorganized into the ranger training brigade and established four ranger training battalions (RTBs). Presently, there are three RTBs:

4th Ranger Training Battalion at Fort Benning, Georgia; 5th Ranger Training Battalion at Dahlonega, Georgia; and 6th Ranger Training Battalion at Eglin Air Force Base, Florida.

Once a soldier completes basic training, advanced individual training, and airborne school, the next training step is the ranger indoctrination program (RIP), a three-week program for enlisted soldiers grades E-1 to E-4. The mission of the ranger training detachment (RTD) conducting RIP is to prepare, assess, and select the soldiers for service in the 75th Ranger Regiment. RIP not only provides the soldier with the tactical skills to function as a member of a ranger squad, but also eliminates the weak and unmotivated. Unfortunately, the rest of the RIP class suffers from the mistakes of the unmotivated. RIP instructors are noncommissioned officers who are carefully chosen from the 75th Ranger Regiment, and they have firsthand knowledge of what it's like to be a ranger squad member. They know that the ranger squad is only as strong as its weakest member. Weakness in body, mind, or spirit will cost lives. It may appear that the instructor cadre implements punishments when soldiers make mistakes and punishments when soldiers perform well. It is difficult to determine if anyone performs well at RIP; but any soldier who is properly motivated can pass RIP and become a U.S. Army Ranger.

Upon assignment to the 75th Ranger Regiment for the RIP course, Rangers are graded on the army physical fitness test (APFT). As a standard, each Ranger must receive a minimum of 70 points in each of three areas according to the 17–21 age group requirements, regardless of their age. The three events are the pushups, sit-ups, and 2-mile run. The ranger physical fitness test also includes a pull-up event. Rangers must complete two of three road marches, one of which must be a 10-mile road march. The candidate must successfully pass the combat water survival test (CWST), which includes underwater equipment removal, a 15-meter swim, and a blind drop during which blindfolded students fall backward into the water. A student must score 70 percent or better in both the ranger first-response exam and a critical skills test, which covers land navigation, marksmanship, and the 12-page blue book of ranger standards, army policy, and ranger history.

At the RIP graduation, the ranger enlistee is awarded a tan beret. These graduates are assigned to one of the three ranger battalions or to the 75th Regimental Headquarters. The graduate is permitted to sew the scroll of his assigned battalion onto his uniform.

Soldiers of grades E-5 and above train to become Rangers through the ranger orientation program (ROP), which is also managed and conducted by the ranger training detachment at Fort Benning, Georgia. Upon ROP graduation, the noncommissioned officer reports directly to the pre-ranger cadre to begin in the next pre-ranger course. The physical challenges in ROP will take a backseat compared to what lies ahead in the pre-ranger course. Before reporting to a ranger battalion, each NCO must earn the elusive black-and-gold tab of ranger school.

The ranger regiment sets its standards above the army's requirements. The armed services vocational aptitude battery (ASVAB) is part of the qualification process for the armed services. It measures knowledge and ability in 10 areas, from math to electronics. A score of 110 on the general test portion of the ASVAB is required. The soldier's overall score, reflecting a compilation of all 10 segments, must be at least 50.

There are specific medical health fitness standards for airborne and ranger training in addition to the standard army entry requirements. For example, the applicant must demonstrate nothing less than full strength, stability, and range of motion for all joints. There must not be a history of vertigo, persistent tinnitus (ringing or buzzing) in the ear, or limited movement of the eardrum. Each soldier receives an electrocardiogram (EKG). Prospective airborne or ranger soldiers must be able to identify the colors red and green. Distant visual acuity must be correctable to 20/20 in one eye and at least 20/100 in the other eye. Lung function must be normal. Chest X-rays are sometimes conducted. Chronic motion sickness, a fear of flying, attempted suicide, or a history of psychosis would exclude soldiers from airborne or ranger training. Soldiers must exhibit normal emotional responses to stressful situations and demonstrate emotional stability. Functions of the head, neck, and spine must be normal, as the physical demands of airborne and ranger training will test the strength of these areas. It is vital for the individual's life and for the lives of others around him that he be in top physical condition.

Although Rangers are hardly typical, the law of common averages has emerged among the elite core. With an average age of 24, these men generally score 275 out of 300 on the army physical fitness test. The typical Ranger is 69 inches tall and weighs 174 pounds. Fewer than half of all Rangers are married. They average 1 3/4 child. Most Rangers have attended some college, and approximately half are ranger tab qualified. Today's Ranger averages 4 1/2 years in the armed services.

The U.S. Army maintains the ranger regiment at a high level of readiness. Each battalion can deploy anywhere in the world with 18 hours' notice. Because of the importance the army places on the 75th Ranger Regiment, it must possess a number of capabilities. These capabilities include infiltrating by land, sea, and air; conducting direct-action operations; conducting raids; recovering personnel and special equipment; and conducting conventional or special light-infantry operations.

Life in the Ranger Regiment

All Rangers are taught raids, ambushes, and reconnaissance actions at squad and platoon levels. Combat leaders are experts in patrolling and surviving. Not only must they know these skills, but they must also teach them to their subordinates. Rangers train year-round in various terrains, climates, and weather conditions, and training takes place day or night. Rehearsing tactics in the training environment allows Rangers to learn from their mistakes, and to avoid making the same mistake twice. Rangers will rehearse a mission until it becomes instinctive: Rehearse in day, execute mission at night. Surprise and shock are two of a Ranger's greatest weapons.

To maintain readiness, Rangers train constantly. Their training encompasses Arctic, jungle, desert, amphibious, and mountain operations. The philosophy of the 75th Ranger Regiment includes performance-oriented training emphasizing tough standards and a focus on realism and live-fire exercises, while concentrating on the basics and safety. Training at night, during adverse weather, or on difficult terrain multiplies the benefits of training events. Throughout training, Rangers are taught to expect the unexpected.

Out of all the army's regular and special operations units, the ranger regiment routinely employs the most intense and grueling physical training regimen. Rangers are the only unit that mandates physical training five days per week, 48 weeks a year. The opportunities to train exceed that of other units. Rangers are allotted more training time and financial resources as well as overseas deployment and off-post training opportunities. They use state-of-the-art equipment and developing technological systems. Selection rates for promotion, schooling, and command positions are higher than army averages. Ranger units have the highest percentage of noncommissioned officers who later become officers in the army. Rangers have the personal and professional satisfaction of contributing to the finest and most elite regiment in the army.

The mission of ranger school is to conduct ranger and long-range surveillance leader courses to further develop the combat arms skills of officer and enlisted volunteers eligible for assignment to units whose primary mission is to engage in close-combat, direct-fire battle. Ranger school purports that it is not a leadership course, and that any leadership skills derived from its training are a secondary benefit.

Troop-leading procedures help a leader to prepare his unit to accomplish a tactical combat mission. This process may be studied in books, but it is the practical implementation of planning each and every detail that truly trains a leader how to prepare the men and resources. In a ranger battalion, Rangers learn from each other through the do-as-I-do method. Enlisted Rangers learn many troop-leading procedures by observing the leaders of their missions.

The ranger school course philosophy centers around the relationship between human potential and human effort exerted. Ranger instructors realize that the individual comfort zone for effort is less than 25 percent of true human potential. The ranger school student self-imposes enough effort to reach 50 percent of total human potential. The ranger school course imposes a stress level that stretches the students to reach 75 percent of their possible potential. Reaching the maximum of 100 percent human potential would mean total exertion, or death. Ranger school instructors are well trained and experienced in evaluating the level of each student's potential, stress threshold, and exerted effort. Since the ranger course's introduction in 1951, ranger instructors have trained over 35,000 students from U.S. armed forces and military personnel from some 60 allied countries.

The ranger training brigade (RTB) conducts the ranger school in three phases at Camp Darby and Camp Rogers,

Daylight jumps are rare for Rangers in the regiment. The darkness of night helps conceal air operations to achieve the needed element of surprise. Rangers are most vulnerable while drifting to the ground with their weapons stowed for air operations. Quick action on the ground is a must.

"Work as a team and get though the course and graduate. You can't do it alone," admonishes a ranger school instructor. Rangers learn teamwork and leadership skills and return to their units with knowledge and experience. The bond a Ranger forms at ranger school with his assigned ranger buddy can last a lifetime.

located at Fort Benning near Columbus, Georgia; Camp Merrill, located near Dahlonega, Georgia; and Camp Rudder, located at Eglin Air Force Base near Fort Walton, Florida. The Benning phase takes place at brigade headquarters at Camps Darby and Rogers with an estimated 44 instructors. The 5th Ranger Training Brigade at Camp Merrill has approximately 162 ranger instructors who conduct the mountain phase. Camp Rudder's 6th Ranger Training Brigade has 170 instructors and hosts the Florida phase. The course's 61 days are divided among the three phases: Benning phase for 20 days, mountain phase for 21 days, and Florida phase for 18 days. The remaining two days are consumed by travel between the phases, maintenance, in/out processing, and graduation. The ranger training brigade will train for 348 days out of the calendar year; 310 of these are considered high-risk training days.

The 61 long and rigorous days of ranger school cause the student's body to weaken as the course progresses, making mental toughness essential. Ranger school students carry a 35- to 55-pound Alice pack and conduct tactical foot movements of 200-plus miles over the span of the course. They eat no more than 2,200 calories a day and consume every calorie, and then some. The average soldier burns 2,800 to 3,200 calories daily, and it's common for a student to lose 20 to 30 pounds during training. Since these men average 19.6 hours of training each day seven days a week, the ranger student can expect four or less hours of sleep each night. The highest attrition occurs during ranger assessment phase (RAP) week, which includes the army physical fitness test (APFT), combat water survival test (CWST), 5-mile run, and land navigation test.

A typical ranger school class of 250 students generally earns an APFT score of 280 or above, which exceeds the minimum 210-point requirement. Student ages range from 19 to 27 years, with an average 2.3 years of military experience. Approximately 40 percent of a typical ranger class consists of officers, while the remaining 60 percent is enlisted and noncommissioned officers. Soldiers typically need a rank of specialist (E-4) or above to enroll in ranger school, but those having a private first class (E-3) rank and 12 months of service in the ranger regiment or battalion can be granted a school slot. Typically, 40 percent of a ranger class graduates with their original class.

The attrition rate in ranger school for battalion rangers is less than 10 percent, due in part to the constant military training that Rangers undergo on a daily basis. It also may be the result of pre-ranger school—one month of physical conditioning and

After several days of field training in the hot summer conditions of Fort Benning, Georgia, a 3rd Battalion Ranger needs an IV to replace critical fluids lost from extreme physical exertion. Every battalion has medical personnel, including a battalion surgeon.

training in basic skills such as patrolling and ambushes for battalion rangers in which students are given ample food and sleep.

Specialized Training

Ranger regiment training is chronic and pervasive, consuming and permeating each individual and the unit on every level. A Ranger knows that in order to fully embrace the Ranger Creed, professional development is a must. Earning the ranger tab is not the final stop. Individuals expand their skills and knowledge by attending other schools and training as well. Specific and specialized schools provide greater in-depth training and practical application that is not provided at the ranger battalion or 75th Ranger Regiment level.

One such school, called survival, evasion, resistance, escape (SERE), trains the Ranger to survive off the land if lost or separated from his unit. Since Rangers operate behind enemy lines, separation from the unit within enemy territory is possible. SERE training is conducted at the Colonel James N. Rowe Training Facility at Camp MacKall near Fort Bragg, North Carolina. General survival skills are taught to some extent at the ranger battalion level, and SERE training provides the student with the opportunity to apply survival skills to worldwide environments. The 19-day school concludes with an evasion exercise in which the student experiences physical and mental stress that tests his endurance, resolve, and techniques. The self-sufficient and resourceful student is the one most likely to graduate

Sniper school students are experts in their weapons systems and are familiar with other domestic and foreign sniper weapon systems. Classes are limited to fewer than 25 students to maintain an instructor-to-student ratio of 1:4 for effective training. Sniper school graduates are infinitely precise. At a distance of 2,000 meters, snipers can hit targeted personnel standing directly beside a noncombatant.

from this course and survive if ever placed in a captive situation.

The U.S. Army pathfinder school trains students in a variety of skills to prepare for arriving troops via airborne insertion. The three-week school is held at Fort Benning, Georgia. Today's pathfinders are trained in airborne, small-boat, vehicle, foot, and sometimes free-fall infiltration techniques. Pathfinders may be expected to coordinate aircraft movement, control parachute drops of personnel and equipment, conduct sling-load operations, and provide initial weather information to commanders. Students hone their navigational skills both with and without the use of modern technology or dismounted navigation. Furthermore, they provide basic air traffic control techniques and navigational

assistance to airborne operations. Pathfinder students establish, mark, and operate helicopter landing and parachute drop zones for the day and nighttime. They survey the site and provide security. They learn drop zone marking techniques for the follow-on forces, and the pathfinder must communicate to the aviator the proper information so the parachutists are released over the drop zone at the appropriate time.

Special operation target interdiction course (SOTIC) is more commonly referred to as sniper school. The mission of the U.S. Army SOTIC is to train volunteers to engage selected point targets with precision rifle fire from a long-range concealed position. During this six-week course at Fort Bragg, North

The SR25 Stoner sniper rifle fires 7.62mm ammunition and is deadly accurate up to 1,800 meters. A sniper's attention to detail results in success, and he must use all five senses to remain acutely aware of his environment. Snipers are on alert to both detect and remain undetected.

Carolina, students are taught advanced rifle marksmanship and sniper marksmanship with the M24 sniper weapon system, a single-shot bolt-action rifle with a 7.62mm round. Sniper students learn to integrate available technology by using the rifle with its scope, a spotting scope, binoculars, and night-vision equipment. The student learns camouflage techniques, concealed movement, observation techniques, target detection, field craft, and range estimation. These key skill areas, when combined with expert marksmanship, ensure maximum engagement of targets.

The mission of the U.S. Army jumpmaster school is to train personnel to coordinate and execute a combat-equipped airborne insertion. This entails the proper attaching, jumping, and releasing of personnel and combat and individual equipment. The four-week-long free-fall parachutists' course at Fort Bragg, North

Carolina, is designed to teach the skills needed for high-altitude airborne operations. This course is more commonly known as HALO (high-altitude, low-opening) school.

The U.S. Army combat diver's school, or combat diver qualification course (CDQC), is best known as scuba school and is one of the toughest schools in the army. Scuba school's objective is to train personnel as qualified military combat divers. These divers perform water operations to include day and night ocean dives, deep dives, and open-circuit swims. Students are evaluated on 1,500-meter and 3,000-meter navigation dives. To accomplish these water operations, the diver must learn diving physics and related injuries, marine hazards, tides and currents, dive tables, and submarine lock-in/lock-out procedures. The water infiltration course (WIC)

The weapons squad leader from the 1st Ranger Battalion helps direct fire onto the objective. The primary job of the assistant gunner is to feed ammunition into the M240 machine gun, help the gunner locate targets, and direct the gunner to these targets. The assistant gunner is also responsible for changing the barrels of the weapon when it becomes too hot to prevent damage to the barrel.

was more recently added and consists of Zodiac operations and navigation, surface swims, Klepper operations, and waterproofing gear.

Combat experience and lessons learned in the training environment have resulted in key principles that ensure successful military operations on urbanized terrain (MOUT). Many coincide with ranger principles of operation, which make ranger units ideal for urban operations and missions. The element of surprise is the first MOUT principle, as the force strikes the enemy at a time and place and in a manner for which the enemy is unprepared. Security is maintained during all phases of the operation, in all directions and for the force's duration in the urban environment. The urban setting is four-dimensional—height, depth, width, and subterranean. The ranger element never permits the enemy to acquire an unexpected advantage and use its element of surprise. Clear,

concise, uncomplicated plans ensure that everyone understands the details of the mission. The MOUT force plans and prepares for the worst, and rehearses everything. The rate of military action is paramount to success. The force moves in a careful hurry and never moves faster than it can accurately engage targets. The final principle in the urban environment is that military action eliminates the enemy with sudden, violent, explosive force. Strong force combined with speed yields a surprise and greatly reduces the opportunity for the enemy's physical and mental reaction.

The Joint Readiness Training Center (JRTC) at Fort Polk, Louisiana, houses the military operations on urbanized terrain (MOUT) complex, which boasts a one-of-a-kind state-of-the-art training facility. The purpose of these facilities is to provide realistic training in third-world and urban-warfare scenarios. These facilities expand the training foundation for light infantry

During the best ranger competition, a participant releases himself from a pulley on the slide for life. Rangers can reach up to 50 miles per hour on the slide, and good entry technique is valuable when hitting the water at such a high speed. The Ranger will bruise if he enters the water at the wrong angle.

and special operations forces. Consisting of three facilities—a mock city, an airfield facility, and a military compound—the MOUT complex trains soldiers to conduct urban environment missions while minimizing or eliminating civilian casualties and collateral damage. Each site within the complex can be used as separate objectives or simultaneously. Each ranger battalion attends at least one JRTC rotation annually.

The ranger force is normally employed as part of a joint special operations task force (JSOTF), and provides a strategically responsive global strike force with highly lethal ground combat capability. It can serve as a flexible deterrent option to demonstrate the United States' resolve by immediately committing military power on land into a threatened area. It can also conduct offensive direct-action (DA) operations against targets of strategic or operational value to achieve theater campaign or major operational objectives. Ranger offensive operations include seizing airfields and other key facilities, performing raids, conducting air movement operations using

A Ranger radio operator swiftly moves off the drop zone at Fort Benning's Fryer Drop Zone in the hot Georgian summer. Most Ranger airborne operations are conducted during the hours of limited visibility to avoid detection.

special operations aviation, and evacuating noncombatants. These operations are characterized by speed, surprise, and violent execution.

In a combat situation, special operations forces such as Rangers depend on the U.S. Air Force for airlift, close air support, and resupply. Likewise, Rangers can expect to operate with heavy armor units equipped with tanks and armored personnel carriers. JRTC exercises integrate the special operations forces with air force, other military, and civilian personnel to replicate realistic scenarios. JRTC's training exercises improve the technical and tactical proficiencies of individual soldiers, their teams and units, and the armed services as a collective whole.

Special Operations Command

Several special operations units fall under the command of U.S. Army Special Operations Command, including the 75th Ranger Regiment. Others include the Special Operations Support Command (Airborne), 160th Special Operations Aviation Regiment (Airborne), Special Forces Command (Airborne) Special Forces Groups, Civil Affairs, and Psychological Operations Command (Airborne).

With time and lessons learned, U.S. Army leadership has now realized that the value provided by small units of well-trained men on the battlefield can greatly exceed the cost of equipment and training. To demonstrate this commitment, the army established the 1st Special Operations Command

Rangers practice close-quart combat firing techniques at Dodge City, an array of structures at Fort Bragg, North Carolina, built for training purposes. Rangers spend countless hours shooting and working on room-clearing techniques. These operations are rehearsed in both daylight and night conditions.

(Airborne) on October 1, 1983, at Fort Bragg, North Carolina. The mission of the U.S. Army Special Operations Command (SOCOM) was to organize, train, educate, man, equip, fund, administer, mobilize, deploy, and sustain army special operations forces to successfully conduct worldwide special operations across the range of military operations in support of regional combatant commanders, American ambassadors, and other agencies as directed.

On December 1, 1989, the army reorganized and activated the U.S. Army Special Operations Command (USASOC), the army's sixteenth major command. USASOC commands all army special operations units with the exception of two special forces groups and one aviation battalion in the national guard. Although the command was reorganized, its mission remained intact. USASOC is the focal point of doctrine, training, operations, and support for the army special operations forces community. It gives the diverse elements of special operations the unity of purpose and guidance necessary for modern warfare. It is a vital part of the recently established joint special operations headquarters, the U.S. Special Operations Command (USSOCOM) at MacDill Air Force Base, Florida.

The flexibility of the ranger force requires that it perform under various command structures. The force can work unilaterally under a corps, as a part of a joint special operations task force (JSOTF), or as an army component in a joint task force. Historically, it has been common for the ranger force to conduct operations as part of a JSOTF and then become the operational control for a joint task force to conduct special operations/direct-action missions. Interfacing and coordinating efforts with other special operations forces and army units is paramount for the success of the individual missions and overall operations.

Gunner and assistant gunner are preparing to fire another HEAT round at hard targets down range at Fort Stewart, Georgia. The 84mm Carl Gustav antitank weapon can also be used to engage bunkers and moving targets.

The Special Operations Support Command (Airborne), abbreviated SOSCOM, was activated on November 1, 1995, as the newest major subordinate unit in the U.S. Army Special Operations Command. It realigned the command-and-control organizational structure of the following units: 112th Special Operations Signal Battalion (Airborne); 528th Special Operations Support Battalion (Airborne); Materiel Management Center (Airborne); and five Special Operations Theater Support Elements (SOTSE). This organizational structure concentrates support for all army special operations forces units with dedicated and regionally oriented combat and health services, communications planning, overall coordination, and a liaison base. SOSCOM is located at Fort Bragg, North Carolina.

The reorganization left a SOTSE in each of five geographical regions around the world. The SOTSE soldiers are embedded in theaters' army staff, and they plan and coordinate with theater army, SOSCOM, and special operations forces, including the Rangers, to ensure support during operations and training. As a theater army staff member, the knowledge of these officers and noncommissioned officers regarding theater-specific requirements and capabilities assists units in coordinating the theater of operations.

Materiel Management Center provides the Rangers and special operations forces with centralized and integrated management of property, equipment maintenance, logistical automation, and repair parts and supplies.

Specializing in advanced communications and resupply capabilities, members of the 112th Special Operations Signal Battalion (Airborne) and the 528th Special Operations Support Battalion (Airborne) have a challenging mission to support the Rangers. In their respective fields, signal and support soldiers

Captains John S. Serafini and Paul W. Staeheli from Team 11 participate in the action on the slide for life during the best ranger competition at Fort Benning, Georgia. Two-man teams are carefully chosen by their units and are usually allowed duty time to train. The event has grown in popularity and is now covered by networks such as ESPN.

provide supplies, maintenance, equipment, and expertise, allowing special operation forces to shoot, move, and communicate on a continuous basis. Because the Rangers use items unique to their missions, soldiers assigned to the 112th and 528th units are taught to operate and maintain a vast array of specialized equipment not normally used by other units in the armed forces. To meet the needs of the Rangers, the two battalions have developed logistical and signal platforms that are deployable on a moment's notice. Rangers are on the move, and their support elements must be as well. Soldiers assigned to the 112th and 528th units are airborne qualified.

The 112th Signal Battalion integrates the theater of special operations command (TSOC), which are attached to each TSOC at their home stations. When deployed, the 112th establishes communications elements at the forward-operating base (FOB) level and at the joint special operations task force (JSOTF) level. The ranger units provide the spokes of the communications network, but the 112th provides the hubs. The hub is crucial, as it then connects to the satellite for global positioning.

Air Assets

The 75th Ranger Regiment displays expansive battlefield diversity, conducting airborne and air assaults in harrowing mountain infiltrations, complex urban raids, and rescue operations. An extensive array of technologically advanced support elements, equipment, and training resources assists the Rangers in achieving their missions. No asset is quite as instrumental in this task as the 160th Special Operations Aviation Regiment (Airborne), or 160th SOAR(A), more commonly referred to as Task Force 160. Without Task Force 160, Rangers would not have the means to infiltrate enemy lines, receive quick-fire support, or be rescued. Many of the successes enjoyed by the 75th Ranger Regiment throughout its history and during the present global war on terrorism are linked directly to the consistent relationship it has with Task Force 160.

The 160th SOAR(A) battalions are organized to address the operational needs of the special operations unit they support, according to the expected theater of operations, type of mission, and level of conflict. The 160th possesses a variety of capable aircraft, including the MH-60 Black Hawk medium-utility helicopters, MH-47 Chinook heavy helicopters, and A/MH-6 Little Bird special operations helicopters. The 160th SOAR(A) keeps its aircraft ready to deploy in a four-hour notice.

Task Force 160, nicknamed the "night stalkers," has responded to the increased demand for elite, highly trained special operations aviation assets and has earned a solid reputation in the special operations community as the unit that is always at the right place, at the right time, and with the right assets. The motto of the 160th SOAR(A) is simply, "night stalkers don't quit." Consistent with their special operations counterparts, Task Force 160 continues its missions despite bad weather, equipment failure, or heavy enemy resistance.

The AH-6 and MH-6 Little Birds, MH-60 Black Hawks, and MH-47 Chinooks of the 160th SOAR(A) insert, extract, and support special operations forces behind enemy lines or within hostile areas. If the situation dictates insertion and extraction of troops by force, Task Force 160 employs accurate helicopter attack capabilities and precise helicopter lifts. They put troops in or take them out of harm's way within 30 seconds of the scheduled time. Army Rangers and Navy SEAL teams are the primary recipients of the night stalkers' specialized aviation tactics and techniques, reliable air support, security, and resources.

Headquartered at Fort Campbell, Kentucky, the 160th SOAR(A) includes the 1st and 2nd Battalions and Special Operations Training Company stationed at Fort Campbell, and the 3rd Battalion at Hunter Army Airfield near Savannah, Georgia. The 160th SOAR(A) also activated a separate detachment and incorporated one national guard battalion. This organizational structure allows the 160th SOAR(A) Regiment to quickly tailor its unique assets to meet mission requirements of special operations forces.

Chapter 3

CENTRAL AMERICA

The M24 sniper weapon system uses a Remington 700 bolt-action rifle with a Leopold Mark IV 10-power scope. Snipers are well trained in stalking, concealment, and other movement techniques. Some snipers will avoid certain foods to prevent emitting a detectable odor. They are masters at moving silently without detection.

Invasion of Grenada

Balmy breezes and lush tropical foliage grace the Caribbean island of Grenada. Sandy white beaches surround steep hilltops. The former British Commonwealth is the smallest independent country in the Western Hemisphere. Problems in the island paradise began brewing in 1979, when a bloodless coup placed the pro-Marxist leader Maurice Bishop as the prime minister of Grenada. Bishop's position strengthened ties between Grenada and communist nations such as Cuba and the Soviet Union.

On October 13, 1983, President Ronald Reagan learned of greater trouble in Grenada, and the situation rapidly escalated. Deputy Prime Minister Bernard Coard, a communist leader backed by the Grenadian Army, had deposed Prime Minister Bishop and established military rule. On October 19, 1983,

Bishop was murdered during a power struggle among men of his own movement. Bishop had reportedly been working to make Grenada a socialist country and a tourist destination. Especially disconcerting to President Reagan was the presence of Cuban construction workers, laborers, and military personnel building a 10,000-foot airstrip on Grenada. Bishop claimed the purpose of the airstrip was to allow commercial jets to land, thus building tourism commerce on the island nation. But with the communist Coard in power, it was feared that the airstrip's purpose was to allow military transport planes loaded with arms from nearby Cuba to be transported to Central American insurgents.

After the coup placing Coard in power, there was violence and anarchy in Grenada. Martial law was established, and a

With a huge explosion from several sticks of C4 placed in the water, onlookers observe a spectacular finish to a demonstration for VIPs and family members attending ranger school graduation at Victory Pond, Fort Benning. The Ranger falling has just let go of the slide for life as the demolition was detonated, creating a huge wall of water.

Ready for war, a ranger squad leader and his squad prepare to engage the enemy in a mountain environment and clear rooms with targets as a training mission.

Each member of the squad has communication with the squad leader. With lightning speed, the squad will move and work rapidly to secure the objective.

After sliding down the slide for life during the best ranger competition, a participant takes a second to compose himself and then cheer on his teammate. If either man on the team is unable to continue, the team is disqualified. The non-stop competition lasts for two days.

shoot-on-sight curfew was placed into effect. The breakdown in civil order threatened the safety and lives of the 800 American medical students who were enrolled and in residence at St. George's School of Medicine.

In October, 1983, the Rangers were instrumentally involved in the restoration of democracy in Grenada. Rangers train to respond with little notice, and preparation for the invasion of Grenada was no different. The invasion, code-named Operation Urgent Fury, cited several objectives. The first was to secure

Point Salines airfield, located on the island's southwestern point. Rangers were then to secure the medical college's True Blue Campus at Salines. Finally, the Rangers were to take the army camp at Calivigny.

Within hours of receiving orders, 1st Ranger Battalion assembled at Saber Hall at Hunter Army Airfield, Georgia, and prepared to board air force C-130s for the flight to Grenada.

Rangers are trained to expect the unexpected because things do not always go as planned. Such was the case with the

The Javelin is an essential and significant ranger weapon system. With two parts, the warhead and the optics, it is a one-time-fire weapon, but the sight and optics can be recovered and used again.

Rangers from the 1st Ranger Battalion conduct military operations on urbanized terrain (MOUT) training at Hunter Army Airfield in Savannah, Georgia. The shoot house is named after 1st Battalion Ranger Specialist Marc A. Anderson, killed in action while fighting the Taliban and al Qaeda during Operation Anaconda in Afghanistan, March 4, 2002. Rangers never forget their fallen comrades or their comrades' families.

invasion of Grenada. A navy SEAL team was unable to get ashore and couldn't provide necessary intelligence on the Point Salines airfield. The lead aircraft experienced problems with inertial navigation equipment. Communications to the Rangers were passed through air force communications, causing a delay. This altered the time of the invasion, originally scheduled during darkness, to early morning light.

While in the air, the Rangers were notified that photographic intelligence indicated obstructions on the airfield. Instead of landing at the airfield as planned, the Rangers would jump at Salines to clear the runway. The Rangers had originally been told to prepare their harness, rucksack, and main and reserve parachutes. These items were placed in kit bags and moved forward in the aircraft to facilitate off-loading troops and cargo after landing. Before long, the loadmasters were yelling, "Only 30 minutes fuel left. Rangers are fighting. Jump in 20 minutes."

But 20 minutes is not enough time for a jumpmaster to check each man's equipment. Buddy rigging was employed as the

Rangers pull security after being dropped off by a Black Hawk helicopter in the mountain phase of ranger school. The students will move to the wood line and into the woods for a few steps to pull a listening halt and observe if any enemies are in the area. A listening halt allows their hearing to adjust from the deafening whir of the rotors to the quiet conditions.

Rangers re-rigged for the airborne drop, pulled on parachutes, and unpacked nonessential equipment. As standard, rucksacks were hooked under the reserve parachute and weapons were strapped to the left side.

Aboard the lead C-130 aircraft, navigation equipment failure and rain squalls interfered with the approach, and the aircraft became inoperable. This meant that if the Rangers were deployed from the aircraft in changed order, the runway clearing team would not be the first on the field. The Rangers requested to implement their contingency plan: a mass parachute assault. With a mass assault, the order of exit from the aircraft would be affected, but all necessary contingencies to secure the airfield would be present. The air force, however, declined to conduct a mass parachute drop.

At 0534 on October 25, 1983, a platoon from B Company, 1st Ranger Battalion, and the Battalion Tactical

Rangers train for the expert
infantryman's badge (EIB)
while performing CPR on a
mannequin. Rangers master
first aid and other life-saving
measures, as any Ranger may
have to perform life-saving
first aid to a wounded team
member while in combat.

The inside of an objective hit by the 1st Ranger Battalion is riddled with bullet holes. The uniforms inside the objective are filled with balloons and hung in various locations throughout the building to represent the enemy. All the balloons must be shot or punctured to simulate a kill. Prior to the training mission, a team constructs the objective.

Operations Center (TOC) began dropping at Salines. A portion of A Company followed almost 25 minutes later. Over a half hour later, the rest of A Company arrived. It was 0634. The remaining men landed on the ground at 0705, approximately 1 1/2 hours after the first drops of 1st Battalion at the Salines airfield. The men conducted a static-line jump from 500 feet and were in the air no more than 15 seconds. Water bordered the airfield to the north and south, making the drop zone very narrow. The airfield was so far southwest on the island, that while the jumpmaster was preparing the men, all that could be seen was water below.

The Rangers assembled on the east end of the runway. They were short C Company, which had been sent with 60 special operations troops to take the Richmond Hill Prison.

Daylight had broken. Shortly after 0700, the 2nd Ranger Battalion began its airdrop and completed it in much less time. During this parachute drop, one Ranger broke his leg, and another Ranger was dragged against the tail of the plane by a tangled static line as he exited the aircraft. He was hauled safely back aboard the aircraft. The 2nd Ranger Battalion assembled on the west end of the airfield.

Once on the ground, the 1st Battalion men were not under effective fire and began to clear the runway of trucks and bull-

Moving through a water-filled trench along the objective, 1st Battalion Rangers head to the checkpoint to link up with the incoming extraction helicopters. In a hostile combat situation, helicopters can only remain on the ground for a limited period of time, as they are more vulnerable to attack when on land. The support elements will be the last to withdraw.

dozers placed there by Cubans to obstruct entry. Some of the vehicles had the keys left in them, while others were hot-wired and driven away. Always resourceful, the Rangers used available means—a Cuban bulldozer—to clear the runway of debris. With this machine, the Rangers flattened the stakes driven into the ground with wires between them and pushed aside the drums placed on the runway. For 15 minutes there was no enemy fire, and the Rangers worked quickly and without interruption.

By 1000, the 1st Battalion's A Company had its second platoon at the True Blue Campus, securing the area and safety of the medical students. A Company's first and third platoons moved north of the runway. In the airfield's center, B Company moved north and held the high ground not far from the Cuban headquarters. The 2nd Battalion was quick to move and complete its part. The men of the 2nd Battalion cleared the area west of the airfield and the area north of their drop zone all the way to Canoe Bay. The airfield was secure. The C-130s returned from their refueling point in Barbados to unload equipment that was not air-dropped, including jeeps, motorcycles, and Hughes 500 Defender helicopters.

Eight hours after landing, the commander of B Company, 2nd Battalion, was notified that two of his

Rangers keep 5 meters of separation between men. That is the basic kill radius for a hand grenade and keeps the Rangers from bunching up to create a target. It also prevents one bullet from hitting two men. Road marching without headgear increases the Rangers' comfort in hot climates.

Waiting for targets to appear after low crawling through 20 yards of barbed wire will get your blood pumping. The blood pounds in the Ranger's ears as he waits and waits. Shooting too soon may give away his position prematurely.

Rangers were missing near their positions. Determining that the missing men must be near a building that lay between B Company and the Cuban positions, the company commander sent forth a Cuban construction worker with an 11-man ranger squad under a flag of truce. While the Rangers remained outside the building, the Cuban entered and spoke with those inside. The building's occupants agreed to a truce and return of the Rangers in exchange for medical treatment for the Cuban wounded. Two Rangers and 17 wounded Cubans were evacuated and treated for their wounds. Afterward, the ranger commander called for the Cubans to surrender, and 80 to 100 responded favorably.

After a brief fight, the remaining Cubans in the building surrendered to the 82nd Airborne troops.

At 1530 that afternoon, Cubans launched a counterattack against A Company, 1st Battalion, that consisted of three BTR-60 armored personnel carriers. These large, eight-wheeled vehicles moved through the second platoon's firing positions and fired toward the secured runway. The Rangers counterfired with rifles, M60 mortars, light antitank weapons (LAWs), and Carl Gustav recoilless rifles. Two of the BTRs crashed into each other when the first one halted, and both were disabled. The third BTR hastily retreated as it was hit by the Rangers' artillery fire. It was then destroyed by an AC-130 Spectre gunship.

Preparing for a mission takes time and planning. Key leaders meet to discuss the best plan of attack, and members of a squad are assigned tasks to help prepare for the mission. The Rangers study terrain models and photos of the objective area. Before leaving on a mission, each man must be briefed on the mission's objective and his individual duties.

Members of a squad from the 3rd Ranger Battalion are briefed for the mission and question the plan of attack. During an operations order, aspects such as who, what, when, and where will be discussed. The weather maps, modes of transportation, and what each man needs to bring on the mission are communicated to the squad. After the mission's completion, the squad members review their performance in an after-action review (AAR).

By the end of the day, the final invasion activity took place east of the True Blue Campus. The Rangers came under fire from a house perched on a hilltop approximately 1,000 meters east of the runway. An AC-130 Spectre gunship was unavailable, so an A-7 attack plane destroyed the house. In the process, several dud shells landed alarmingly close to the Rangers, who had secured the airfield and True Blue Campus at a cost of five dead and six wounded.

While A and B Companies of 1st Battalion were securing the airfield, their fellow Rangers of C Company, along with 60 special operations soldiers, were tasked with taking over the Richmond Hill Prison, a stronghold for the Cuban forces. Perched on a high ridge with nearly vertical slopes and dense tropical foliage, the prison itself was surrounded by 20-foot-high walls topped with barbed wire. Watchtowers surrounded the prison area.

When arriving to the prison via Black Hawk helicopters, Rangers, special operations forces, and Task Force 160 pilots learned the local defenses were active, with two antiaircraft guns manned on a ridge some 150 feet above the prison. Originally, the Rangers were to fast rope into the area, but helicopters must remain steady during a fast rope operation, making the Rangers

Rangers intently review and discuss the actions on the objective. After reviewing the plan of attack and the routes that will be traveled, a rehearsal will take place to work out and talk about contingency plans. Rangers are accustomed to rehearsing in the daylight and conducting missions at night.

A UH-60 direct-action penetrator (DAP) Black Hawk helicopter provides covering fire from its 7.62mm miniguns as the Rangers fast rope to conduct a raid and prisoner-of-war extraction. This training exercise was conducted at Fort Bragg, North Carolina, by elements of the 2nd Ranger Battalion stationed at Fort Lewis, Washington.

and crews easy targets for engagement by the enemy. The approaching Black Hawk helicopters were brought under fire, making it far too risky and nearly impossible for the Rangers to infiltrate by fast rope. Unfortunately, air support was not possible at the time, since all small aircraft were engaged at the Point Salines airfield.

Nonetheless, the Black Hawks made at least two attempts to bring in and unload troops into the area, but antiaircraft fire hit the American forces. Suppressive fire from the Black Hawks was ineffective. Although some Rangers walked away from the crashed Black Hawks, others were badly hurt and, unfortunately, were not evacuated immediately. Part of the delay

in evacuation seems to have been that army pilots could not land aboard navy ships because they were not qualified to do so, although this requirement was eventually waived.

The Rangers learned at 1030 that same morning that there were American students at the medical college's second campus at Grand Anse. Students reported Cuban forces or guards in the area. A heliborne operation with marine airlift from Guam was planned. Marine Helicopter Squadron 261 would provide the helicopters, with supporting fire from C-130 gunships, additional ships off the coast, and the marines' two remaining Cobra attack helicopters. American suppressive fire was to continue until 20 seconds before the Rangers were committed to the area.

The ranger training department based at Fort Benning, Georgia, is responsible for the demonstrations that the civilians view at ranger school graduations. Graduation is held at Victory Pond, the same place where ranger school begins. Demonstrators show the basics to the observers so they can see some of the training situations the students go though during ranger school.

The Rangers were to fly to the objective in three waves of three CH-46 helicopters each. Each wave of three helicopters would carry about 50 Rangers. Second Battalion, A Company, would go in first, followed by B Company, which would cordon off the campus to prevent outside intervention. C Company would then arrive, locate the students, and pack them into four CH-53 Sea Stallions waiting offshore for the call to make the pickup.

During liftoff, the order of aircraft became confused. Instead of the lead flight having three CH-46 helicopters from A Company, the first wave had one load from A Company and two from B Company. Consequently, the second wave had two from A Company and one from B Company. The first three aircraft missed the designated beach in front of the campus. Despite the mistakes, the Rangers carried out the assigned mission. The circling CH-53 Sea Stallion helicopters were brought in to extract students from the Grand Anse campus, and the CH-46 helicopters returned and extracted the Rangers, completing the entire operation in 26 minutes.

During this operation, there was sporadic small arms fire, but the only serious damage to the helicopters came from overhanging trees along the shore. One helicopter shut down and was abandoned in the surf. The Rangers scrambled out and moved to safety as water poured in. Later, a tree damaged a second helicopter.

After hitting the ground like a ton of rocks, a Ranger from 1st Ranger Battalion places his weapon into operation. Rangers quickly double time off the drop zone and spread over a large area because they are susceptible to enemy fire in the open.

After leaving the beach on the CH-46 helicopters, the Rangers realized that the 11 men sent up as a flank guard had not returned. The men were instructed via radio to move toward positions held by the 82nd Airborne. The 11 Rangers were not certain they could safely enter those lines and decided to use an inflatable boat from a disabled helicopter. Unfortunately, the boat was significantly damaged during the air assault. The Rangers swam alongside the disabled boat, battling surf and tides. They were spotted and retrieved at 2300 that evening and brought to the USS *Caron* lying off the coast.

By October 27, the Calivigny barracks had not yet been secured. Lying about 5 kilometers from the Point Salines airfield, the barracks was reportedly used to house and train Cuban troops. Under the command of Brigade Headquarters from the 82nd Airborne Division, the 2nd Ranger Battalion, with reinforcement from C Company, 1st Ranger Battalion, carried out a full-scale attack on the barracks.

Four waves of four Black Hawks, each carrying a company of men, were to fly low over the sea at 100 knots before heading to the beach. At nearby Salines airfield, the army had in place 17 105mm howitzers. At sea, the USS *Caron* would supply fire support. Spectre gunships and navy A-7s supported the Rangers. A Company, 2nd Battalion, was to land at the southern end of the compound. To the left and right, C Company, 2nd Battalion, was to set down. B Company, 2nd Battalion, was to land in the southeast, assault suspected antiaircraft guns, and

Preparing to perform a right front parachute landing fall (PLF) once making contact with the ground, a Ranger pulls his risers on his right side. All Rangers are airborne qualified and receive their jump wings prior to assignment at the regiment. Rangers from the 75th Ranger Regiment have made several combat jumps in the global war on terrorism.

then rejoin the other companies in the north. C Company, 1st Battalion, waited in reserve to reinforce positions and hold the southern end of the perimeter.

The Black Hawks carrying Rangers came in over the ocean waves, climbing sharply to the top of the cliffs. Traveling at 100 knots, each Black Hawk came in rapid succession. Quickly, the pilots slowed down in order to find the exact landing zone inside the perimeter. The first helicopter put down safely near the southern boundary of the camp. The second Black Hawk followed with a safe landing. The third Black Hawk suffered some damage, spun forward, and smashed into the second helicopter. In the fourth Black Hawk, the pilot and crew saw what was happening and quickly veered a hard right, avoiding the other three aircraft. The fourth Black Hawk landed in a ditch, damaging its tail rotor. Apparently not realizing that the heli-

copter's rotor was damaged, the pilot attempted to move the Black Hawk, which rose sharply, spun forward, and crashed. Within 20 seconds, three Black Hawks were down and disabled. Debris and rotor blades had flown through the air, badly wounding four Rangers and killing three.

A Company regrouped as C Company landed in Black Hawks on large concrete pads on the edge of the compound. B Company, 2nd Battalion, and C Company, 1st Battalion, Rangers landed safely and without incident. The men moved to the objective. They did not incur enemy fire. The Calivigny barracks were deserted. The Rangers found nothing, and that night they slept in the rubble created by the intense bombardment.

In two days, Rangers, army special operations forces, and marines subdued the Cuban and Coard-supportive Grenadian

The Ranger jumping into the water has 550 cord tied from his poncho-wrapped rucksack to his body so the rucksack won't be separated from him. Upon entering the water, the team will swim together to a finish line. Their official finish time will be recorded once they cross the finish line with all personnel and equipment.

forces. The invading forces encountered unexpected heavy anti-aircraft fire and ground resistance by the Cuban soldiers and laborers. The 5,000-strong American force discovered a cache of weapons that could arm 10,000 men that included automatic rifles, machine guns, rocket launchers, antiaircraft guns, howitzers, cannons, armored vehicles, and coastal patrol boats. Out of 800 Cubans, 59 were killed, 25 were wounded, and the rest were returned to Havana upon their surrender. Forty-five Grenadians died, and 337 were wounded. Nineteen American servicemen died during Operation Urgent Fury, and 119 were wounded. Of the 19, eight Rangers paid the ultimate sacrifice. The medical students returned to America unharmed, and the 1st and 2nd Ranger Battalions returned from Grenada to their home duty stations.

By mid-December 1983, an interim advisory council was established to govern Grenada. In December 1984, Herbert A. Blaize, the head of the New National Party, was made prime minister by a parliamentary election.

Invasion of Panama

Manuel Noriega seized control of Panama in 1983 when he became head of the national guard. From this position of power, he built up the military and manipulated elections so that the winning presidents became his puppet leaders. Corruption was widespread under Noriega, and he was able to use his power to imprison and sometimes kill those who opposed him. In 1987, a former officer of the Panamanian defense force publicly accused Noriega of

Rangers Killed in Action—Grenada

Sergeant Randy E. Cline
A Company, 1st Battalion (Ranger), 75th Infantry
Killed in action, October 25, 1983

Sergeant Mark A. Rademacher
A Company, 1st Battalion (Ranger), 75th Infantry
Killed in action, October 25, 1983

Sergeant Phillip S. Grenier
A Company, 2nd Battalion (Ranger), 75th Infantry
Killed in action, October 25, 1983

Private First Class Russell L. Robinson
A Company, 1st Battalion (Ranger), 75th Infantry
Killed in action, October 25, 1983

Sergeant Kevin J. Lannon
A Company, 2nd Battalion (Ranger), 75th Infantry
Killed in action, October 25, 1983

Sergeant Stephen E. Slater
A Company, 2nd Battalion (Ranger), 75th Infantry
Killed in action, October 25, 1983

Private First Class Markin R. Maynard
A Company, 1st Battalion (Ranger), 75th Infantry
Killed in action, October 25, 1983

Specialist Four Mark O. Yamane
A Company, 1st Battalion (Ranger), 75th Infantry
Killed in action, October 25, 1983

cooperating with Colombian drug producers. An unsuccessful Panamanian Defense Force (PDF) coup attempt in October produced bloody outcomes, and opposition leaders were physically beaten. By the fall of 1989, Noriega's regime was barely clinging to power. Distrustful of the PDF, Noriega began to rely on irregular paramilitary units called dignity battalions (DIGBATs).

On December 15, 1989, the Panamanian legislature assembly declared Noriega the president of Panama. The Noriega-led assembly declared that the United States and Panama were in a state of war, making Panama unsafe for U.S. forces and citizens. Service members and dependents were harassed. The next day, Panamanian soldiers killed an unarmed U.S. Marine lieutenant dressed in civilian clothes.

The United States' response was quick and decisive. On December 17, 1989, U.S. President George H. W. Bush ordered troops to Panama. The president announced the United States' aims were to seize Noriega to face drug charges in the United States, protect American lives and property, and restore Panamanian liberties.

From Fort Bragg in North Carolina, and Fort Benning and Fort Stewart in Georgia, forces were alerted, marshaled,

and launched on a fleet of 148 aircraft. Units from the 75th Ranger Regiment and 82nd Airborne Division were scheduled to conduct airborne assaults and strike key objectives at Rio Hato Military Airfield and Torrijos-Tocumen International Airport. Their objectives were to protect American lives, key sites, and facilities; capture and deliver Noriega to an authority; neutralize PDF forces' command and control; restructure the PDF; and support the establishment of a United States–recognized government in Panama.

The entire 75th Ranger Regiment participated in the invasion of Panama on December 20, 1989. The Rangers were tasked with securing the Torrijos-Tocumen International Airport, the Rio Hato Military Airfield, and General Noriega's beach house in their mission, Task Force Red.

At 1800 on December 19, 1989, Task Force Red Tango departed Hunter Army Airfield outside of Savannah, Georgia. At 0100 on December 20, an AC-130 Spectre gunship opened fire on the compound of the Panamanian Defense Force (PDF) 2nd Infantry Company as AH-6 gunships fired on additional targets. Three minutes later, hundreds of Rangers filled the area as four companies conducted a low-level parachute jump onto the tarmac of the airfield. The members of Task Force Red

Left: Rappelling off a tower in the hot sun is good training and builds confidence. During the best ranger competition, participants rapidly descend in a timed event and are awarded points from each event they complete. The rappel begins with a prusik knot climb. Upon reaching the top, the Ranger quickly moves down again to the ground.

In between training, Rangers find a few minutes to rest before the platoon sergeant or squad leader rouses them to conduct more live-fire training. Rangers are masters of sleeping under any condition and in any noisy environment, including on a truck, in a C-130 transport, or directly on the ground.

Tango—1st Battalion, C Company of 3rd Battalion, and Team Gold from Regimental Headquarters—secured Torrijos-Tocumen International Airport. They went to work neutralizing the PDF's 2nd Infantry Company at the airport to secure the area prior to the 82nd Airborne Division's airborne assault 45 minutes later. C Company of 3rd Battalion was to clear and seize the main air terminal. The second and third floors of the terminal were cleared, but the first floor was isolated. The PDF had taken a number of hostages, but after 2 1/2 hours of negotiations, the hostages were released to the Rangers. By 0630 on the morning of December 20, 1989, the Torrijos-Tocumen International Airport was secured. A forward aerial resupply point (FARP) was established to receive incoming aircraft.

On December 28, the men of Task Force Red Tango began reconnaissance-in-force operations in the vicinity of Cerro Azul to pursue the remaining PDF and DIGBAT forces, seize reported weapons caches, and neutralize potential rally points and exfiltration routes to the Panamanian interior. Rangers of the 1st Battalion, C Company of 3rd Battalion, and Team Gold from Regimental Headquarters redeployed on January 3, 1990.

Another ranger element, Task Force Red Romeo, consisted of the 2nd Battalion, A and B Companies of 3rd Battalion, and Team Black of Regimental Headquarters. They departed Lawson Army Air Field at Fort Benning, Georgia, at 1800 on December 19, 1989. Task Force Red Romeo's mission was to seize Rio Hato Military Airfield and neutralize the 6th and 7th PDF Infantry Companies. While Task Force Red Tango

Rangers Killed in Action—Republic of Panama

Staff Sergeant Larry Barnard
B Company, 3rd Battalion, 75th Ranger Regiment
Killed in action, December 20, 1989

Private First Class Roy Brown Jr.
A Company, 3rd Battalion, 75th Ranger Regiment
Killed in action, December 20, 1989

Specialist Phillip Lear
B Company, 2nd Battalion, 75th Ranger Regiment
Killed in action, December 20, 1989

Private First Class James W. Markwell
C Company, 1st Battalion, 75th Ranger Regiment
Killed in action, December 20, 1989

Private First Class John Mark Price
A Company, 2nd Battalion, 75th Ranger Regiment
Killed in action, December 20, 1989

was dropping onto the Torrijos-Tocumen International Airport, Task Force Red Romeo parachuted onto its drop zone from C-130s at Rio Hato Military Airfield. The Rangers encountered heavy antiaircraft fire. Both the 6th and 7th PDF Infantry Companies had been alerted of the invasion and fired on the C-130s with small arms. One Ranger was hit in the back of the head while still in the airplane, but the soldier survived. Five Rangers were killed in the operation. Despite Panamanian resistance, the Rangers assembled, attacked the barracks, and established a perimeter. They swiftly attacked the main air terminal of Rio Hato Military Airfield. At Rio Hato, the Rangers were supported by AC-130 Spectre gunships with technologically advanced target acquisition cameras to find targets in the dark. Within two hours of landing, the Rangers of Task Force Red Romeo accomplished all their missions, secured the area, captured 250 prisoners, and cleared the airfield for transport aircraft to begin landing with supplies and additional equipment. The Rangers then moved into Panama City, where they took the military headquarters of the PDF.

Once the airfields were secure, the Rangers carried out security operations and special operations in support of Joint Task Force (South). Task Force Red Romeo moved to neutralize the Panamanian special forces, known as the mountain troops. Rangers moved from house to house in the compound and through the village where the families of the soldiers lived. Many of the mountain troops were caught trying to shave off their distinctive beards. On the fifth day of the operation, the Rangers

were sent to secure Calle Diez, an area approximately 25 miles from Panama City that was held by Noriega's fierce dignity battalions. The Rangers of Task Force Red Romeo redeployed on January 9 and 10, 1989.

On the first day of the invasion, Noriega took refuge in the Papal Nuncio's residence (Vatican Embassy) in Panama City. General Noriega surrendered to United States authorities on January 3, 1990. He was transported to Miami, where he was tried, convicted, and jailed on drug trafficking charges. General Noriega is currently serving his 40-year prison sentence in Miami. In Panama and France, Noriega was charged with various crimes, including murder, but no lasting efforts were made to have him extradited to stand trial on those charges.

U.S. forces rapidly took over and guarded the power, water, and communications infrastructures, which never went out of service. Rangers guarded buildings such as the Vatican Embassy to ensure that damage wasn't done. Rangers took many photographs of Panamanian and foreign property, aircraft, shops, and houses to show that it was reasonably undamaged, intact, and protected by the U.S. Army.

The Rangers captured 1,014 prisoners of war and over 18,000 arms of various types. Twenty-three U.S. service members, including five Rangers, were killed during this massive invasion. The Rangers incurred 42 wounded, but hundreds from both nations were wounded. An estimated 200 to 300 Panamanian soldiers and paramilitaries were killed in the operation, with approximately 300 Panamanian civilian losses, but the accuracy of these figures is still contested.

Chapter 4

THE MOG

Moving from the line of departure, men from 3rd Ranger Battalion, 75th Ranger Regiment, rehearse and train with blank firing for safety before the live-fire exercise. The blank fire also helps Rangers work on the sectors of fire and moving onto the object by letting the support elements know the location of their platoon.

Rangers are usually limited to operations that are three days long or less, because such short missions don't require resupply. A typical ranger mission might be seizing an airfield for use by the general-purpose forces that are already in transport, or conducting raids on key operational and strategic targets in order to better secure an area. Once the follow-up forces arrive, the Rangers move out.

As a special forces unit, the 75th Ranger Regiment believes and operates on these truths: humans are more important than hardware; quality is better than quantity; special operations forces cannot be mass produced; and competent special operations forces cannot be created after emergencies occur. Training reinforces these truths.

A Starving Nation

After the invasion of Panama in 1989, The next Ranger deployment was in Somalia in 1993 for Operation Restore Hope. The 3rd Ranger Battalion's B Company was deployed from August 26, 1993, to October 21, 1993, to assist the United Nations' forces in establishing order to a desperately corrupt and chaotic nation. A Company of the 3rd Ranger Battalion deployed to Somalia from October 5, 1993, to October 23, 1993, in support of U.N. operations. At civil war since 1977 in a country where violent Somali clansmen commonly conducted killings and beheadings, the Somali government collapsed in 1991. The Rangers took part in seven missions trying to capture Somali National Alliance (SNA) clan leader General Mohammed

A ground mobility vehicle (GMV) with an M2 .50-caliber heavy machine gun provides covering fire for the men in the vehicle as they prepare to dismount. The men will get on line and low crawl under barbed wire as part of a stress fire exercise at Fort Benning with 3rd Ranger Battalion. Eyes and ears are alert as each man observes his sector.

Farah Aidid and his top lieutenants. The nation of Somalia was starving, and Aidid's guerrilla war against UN efforts to feed the Somali people needed to end.

During August and September 1993, the task force conducted six missions into Mogadishu, all of which were tactical successes. On October 3, 1993, B Company and members of Special Forces Operational Detachment—Delta conducted a daylight raid, named Task Force Ranger (TFR), in one of the most dangerous parts of Mogadishu to capture two of Aidid's officers in the

Olympic Hotel. Helicopters carrying assault and blocking forces launched at 1530, and a ground convoy departed three minutes later. Within 10 minutes, the ground forces were at the target location, with the blocking force setting up perimeter positions. The team was successful in capturing these two officers, plus approximately 21 others, and began the extraction process within 20 minutes of the assault's commencement. Humvees were dispatched for the extraction and reached the Olympic Hotel despite an ambush by clansmen of Aidid.

During an exercise with several timed events, Rangers from 3rd Ranger Battalion, 75th Ranger Regiment, drag a 250-pound mannequin over 100 yards from a disabled vehicle to the finish line. Before completing the exercise, they will engage targets with individual weapons. The squad must provide security while dragging the body.

Competitors jump from a Black Hawk during the spot jump event at the best ranger competition at Fort Benning, Georgia. A small area is marked on the drop zone for the jumpers to land on, or at least as close as possible. The team with both jumpers landing closest to the marked area will be given the highest score for that event. The round canopy parachutes lack precision maneuverability, so this event has its challenges.

Rangers Killed in Action—Somalia

Corporal James M. Cavaco
B Company, 3rd Battalion, 75th Ranger Regiment
Killed in action, October 3, 1993

Sergeant Dominick M. Pilla
B Company, 3rd Battalion, 75th Ranger Regiment
Killed in action, October 3, 1993

Sergeant James C. Joyce
B Company, 3rd Battalion, 75th Ranger Regiment
Killed in action, October 3, 1993

Sergeant Lorenzo M. Ruiz
B Company, 3rd Battalion, 75th Ranger Regiment
Killed in action, October 3, 1993

Specialist Richard W. Kowalewski
B Company, 3rd Battalion, 75th Ranger Regiment
Killed in action, October 3, 1993

Corporal James E. Smith
B Company, 3rd Battalion, 75th Ranger Regiment
Killed in action, October 3, 1993

The obstacle course places stress on the individual by making him exert large amounts of energy and pump up his heart rate. Then the Ranger must engage targets with his weapon. Rangers train just as they fight—hard. Training situations are created to simulate combat as much as possible.

Rangers from 1st Ranger Battalion engage hard targets with an 84mm Carl Gustav antitank weapon during a live-fire exercise at Fort Stewart, Georgia. In training, Rangers are only permitted to fire a few rounds a day due to the high level of compression that the body is exposed to, even though this is a recoilless weapon.

One MH-60 Black Hawk was shot down by a rocket-propelled grenade (RPG) and crashed about three blocks from the Olympic Hotel. The Rangers set out to rescue the soldiers in the fallen Black Hawk. One six-man element of the blocking force, an MH-6 Little Bird assault helicopter, and an MH-60 Black Hawk carrying a 15-man combat search and rescue (CSAR) team began rushing to the scene. The MH-6 crew got there first and, although fired upon, they managed to evacuate two wounded soldiers. The six-man blocking element arrived, followed by the CSAR helicopter. As the last two members of the CSAR were sliding down the fast ropes, their MH-60 heli-

copter was hit by an RPG, but the pilot kept it steady while the two Rangers safely reached the ground and then nursed the helicopter back to the airport.

At the first crash site, intense fire from machine guns, hand grenades, and RPGs pinned down the Rangers, who established a perimeter inside the nearby buildings to treat their wounded and wait for extraction. Darkness fell. That evening, a helicopter resupplied the soldiers. Expecting a brief raid mission, the Rangers had been instructed to leave water and provisions behind. Some had run out of ammunition. The Rangers were encircled and received intense direct and indirect enemy fire. For

Rangers from 3rd Ranger Battalion prepare to board a C-141 aircraft for a parachute assault to clear and secure an airfield. Such a mission assignment is commonplace in the ranger battalion. Rangers will secure the area for follow-on forces. Rangers help one another rig and check equipment. Jumpmasters also check rigging. Safety is crucial.

nearly 18 hours, the Rangers stood their ground and delivered devastating firepower, killing an estimated 300 to 600 Somalis. The situation was extremely grave, and clearly, if the Rangers at the first crash site were not rescued by a ground element, they would be overwhelmed by the mob of Somalis.

The situation worsened for the Rangers. Two more Black Hawk helicopters were hit by RPG rounds. One aircraft was hit broadside, but the crew coaxed it to a secured area where they managed a controlled crash landing. The other MH-60 Black Hawk's tail rotor was severed, and the helicopter spun to the ground, crashing less than a mile south of the first downed helicopter. A Somali mob overran this second site and killed everyone except the pilot, Chief Warrant Officer Mike Durant, who they took prisoner. Durant received severe injuries to his back and shattered his leg; he was conscious but immobile.

Delta Force Master Sergeant Gary Gordon and Sergeant First Class Randall Shughart unhesitatingly volunteered to be inserted to protect Durant at the second helicopter's crash site.

Airborne operations are a large part of ranger missions. In the Middle East, Rangers depend a great deal on desert mobility vehicles (DMVs) and special operations air force MH-53J Pave Low helicopters from Task Force 160 to travel to targets and reconnaissance areas of operations. Rangers are so accustomed to airdrops that injuries are kept to a minimum. As soon as the Rangers land, they ready their weapons and proceed to link up with their squad.

After hitting the ground from a jump, Rangers de-rig equipment and place the parachute in an aviator's kit bag. During training, the parachute is brought to a turn-in point that is usually scattered down the middle of the drop zone or along an adjacent road. During a combat mission, the silk parachute is discarded and left on the drop zone.

Rangers jumping onto a drop zone is a very common sight. A mass tactical jump is the insertion stage at the beginning of the mission. Those with crew-served weapon systems are the first to exit the aircraft so they can get on the ground and quickly engage the enemy and provide firepower to cover the remaining jumpers. In the event the aircraft takes enemy fire and the "stick," or remaining jumpers, must cease exiting, those with the most casualty-producing weapons are on the ground and able to carry on with the mission.

After landing on the drop zone, a Ranger from 1st Ranger Battalion rolls up the parachute with the suspension lines to be put into his aviator's kit bag. Rangers quickly remove the parachute rigging from their bodies to prevent dragging down the drop zone. Rangers stay low and move fast to get off the drop zone and on with the mission.

Rangers jump with knee pads, elbow pads, and plastic ankle braces to help protect them from jump-related injuries. This Ranger has jumped with an assault pack, which is considerably smaller than the normal ranger rucksack. Rangers have the option to modify the configuration of their rucksacks and some equipment depending on the mission.

All Rangers are airborne qualified and must jump at least every three months to maintain their status. Rangers are paid extra hazardous-duty pay for this qualification. The men are trained by the black hats at the basic airborne course at Fort Benning, Georgia. Three distinctive large towers mark the jump school's location at the base.

Snipers with the special operations command, Gordon and Shughart were inserted on the second approach, 100 meters south of the crash site. They were well aware of the growing number of enemy personnel closing in on the area. Each was equipped with a sniper rifle and a pistol, and, while under intense small-arms fire from the enemy, the men fought their way through a dense maze of shanties and shacks to reach the critically injured crew members. The snipers immediately pulled the pilot from the Black Hawk and established a perimeter. Gordon and Shughart continued protecting the downed crew as their ammunition supply ran low. Shughart continued his protective

fire until he depleted his ammunition and was fatally wounded. Gordon gave ammunition to the pilot and then radioed for help. His own rifle ammunition exhausted, Gordon returned to the wreckage, recovered a rifle with the last five rounds of ammunition and gave it to the pilot with the words "good luck." Then, armed only with his pistol, Gordon continued to fight until he was fatally wounded. The actions of Gordon and Shughart saved the pilot's life, and for their extraordinary heroism and devotion to duty, each was posthumously awarded the Medal of Honor.

With the Somali detainees loaded on trucks, the ground convoy force attempted to reach the first crash site from the

Tape on the helmet, which covers the attachment for night-vision goggles, prevents static lines from cuts in the lines or entanglements. Normally, training jumps are conducted during optimal weather conditions and daylight hours. Combat mission jumps are usually at night, sometimes during less-than-desirable weather. Static lines automatically deploy the Ranger's parachute upon exiting the aircraft.

north. Unable to find it among the narrow, winding alleyways, the convoy came under ambushes, Somali small-arms fire, and RPG fire. The convoy returned to the base at Mogadishu Airport after suffering numerous casualties, losing two 5-ton trucks that were abandoned on the spot, and sustaining significant damage to other vehicles. On the way back to the base, this convoy encountered a second relief convoy that had left the airport in hopes of reaching the second crash site. The determined convoy came under heavy RPG and small-arms fire, yet continued to press forward. When the convoy, commanded by Captain Michael Whetstone, reached the second crash site, Somalis had overrun the site, and there was nothing to recover.

A reinforcement convoy of Rangers, 10th Mountain Division soldiers, SEALs, and Malaysian armored personnel carriers pressed forward to reach the Rangers at the first Black Hawk crash site. The relief force encountered heavy fire en route to their fellow Rangers after several attempts to reach the downed heli-

copter site. Their attempts were complicated by multiple ambushes along the primary route to the downed Black Hawk site. For three hours, the force fought its way in and finally arrived at 0155 on October 4. Commander of the relief force, Lieutenant Colonel David was informed by Captain Drew Meyerowich that the remains of one of the aircraft pilots was trapped in the aircraft, making it extremely difficult to dislodge him. Lieutenant Colonel David reassured the men that they would stay in the objective area until all personnel and remains were recovered. Intensive direct and indirect enemy fire continued. The combined force worked until dawn to free the pilot's body.

All the casualties were loaded onto the Malaysian armored personnel carriers, and the remainder of the force moved out on foot, with the armored personnel carriers providing rolling cover. The run and gun movement, known as the Mogadishu mile, began at 0542. In support, AH-6 attack helicopters circled the convoy and raked across streets with suppressive fire.

The lower jumper has the right of way in the air. If a jumper crosses over another, he may steal his air, causing that jumper to fall to the earth very quickly and dangerously. If this happens at a high enough altitude, it isn't much of a problem, but the closer to the ground it occurs, the more dangerous it becomes.

Medical personnel attend to an injured jumper on the drop zone. Even with all the safety equipment and safety precautions taken by leaders, individual airborne operations are inherently dangerous, and Rangers get hurt or even killed. The medic's initial evaluation indicated that a small bone was broken on the top of the foot. Further medical attention and X-rays are necessary at a hospital in the area. The battalion surgeon must clear an injured Ranger before he can return to airborne operations and duty assignments.

The combat infantryman's badge (CIB) for combat service was presented to the men of the 1st Ranger Battalion for their combat in Afghanistan. The star shows more than one major combat deployment. Such an award is highly prized among the ranger elite and conventional forces. A pin such as this is worn on class A and dress uniforms.

Decorations and pins from schools that Rangers attend: scuba school (lower left); a foreign jump school represented by Uruguay Jump Wings (top center); and jump-master school (top right). The black-and-gold ranger tab is the elusive reward for graduating the ranger course. The colors are subdued for the desert battle dress uniform. The 1st Ranger Battalion scroll dons the unit's red and black colors; the black represents the nighttime operations and the Ranger's deceptiveness; the red symbolizes the unit's speed and aggressiveness. The unit crest (center left) is worn on the Ranger's tan beret.

In a training exercise at Fort Bragg, North Carolina, wounded Rangers are brought to a secure centralized location to receive medical attention while the plan for an extraction is implemented. During this deployment, Rangers use a cleared room as the casualty collection point. Here, they not only get the wounded ready for evacuation, but also mark the dead and assign personnel to carry these bodies. Every possible scenario is rehearsed repeatedly to decrease the possibility of mistakes and uncertainties.

Somalis fired sporadic RPG and small-arms fire at the convoy. Minor wounds were sustained. The convoy arrived at the Pakistani Stadium at 0630 on October 4.

Six Rangers were killed in action, and numerous others were wounded. The night stalkers lost two Black Hawks and five aircrew in the daylight firefight in Mogadishu. The 10th Mountain Division lost one man. A total of 16 Americans paid the ultimate sacrifice; another 83 were wounded. Chief Warrant Officer Mike Durant, who was captured after his Black Hawk was shot down, was released on October 14, 1993.

Numerous accounts, recounts, and documents are available to dissect this operation. Books have been written and a movie was produced, but words and pictures cannot approach an accurate retelling of the horrific situation and heroic actions of all men involved in Mogadishu.

At the Joint Readiness Training Center (JRTC) at Fort Polk, Louisiana, the Shughart–Gordon site is a 29-building mock city that covers a 7-square-kilometer area. It was named after the two Delta Force operators and Medal of Honor recipients who died during Operation Restore Hope in Somalia while defending the second MH-60 Black Hawk crash site. This mock city includes a church, hospital, several multistory buildings, and an underground tunnel or sewer system. Air assault and fast-rope operations can be conducted within this site. Four live-fire buildings permit platoon-sized, live-fire training with short-range training ammunition (SRTA); simunitions; or

Ranger school is one "big smoke" session. Here, a ranger school candidate is carrying his Ranger buddy to the knife-fighting pit during the Benning phase. The students are required to carry a 2-quart canteen for hydration at all times during the summer months.

Switching from black berets to tan created a bit of a stir among the prior-service Rangers. The tan berets now serve as the distinctive visual symbol of the premier light infantry force that is called the Rangers.

A Ranger takes advantage of all training and schooling opportunities. The combat infantryman's badge (CIB) above the jumpmaster wings is worn proudly on the standard battle dress uniform. This Ranger has also graduated from high-altitude, low-opening (HALO) school, represented by the badge under the U.S. Army name tape. HALO school is an airborne insertion school using jumps from a high altitude with a parachute deployment low to the ground. Some Rangers have been awarded stars above their CIBs that show they have participated in combat more than once.

A young Ranger with an M4 carbine rifle complete with a Trijicon advanced compact optical gun (ACOG) sight 4x scope drills on quick response to action. Bringing the weapon up and down several times helps build muscle memory and finally turns into an instinctual response.

plastic paint bullets. The city's water tower acts as a command-and-control facility and observation platform.

Night Stalkers and the Ranger Mission

The 160th Special Operations Aviation Regiment (Airborne), commonly known as Task Force 160, was instrumental October 3–4, 1993, during Task Force Ranger in Somalia. Task Force 160's night stalkers are volunteers. The 160th SOAR(A) seeks the best-qualified aviators and support soldiers available in today's army. Once assigned to the regiment, incoming officers and enlisted soldiers go through basic mission qualification. The officer qualification course lasts 14 weeks, while the enlisted qualification course lasts three weeks. Two other aviator qualification levels exist: fully mission qualified and flight lead. Special operations pilots and soldiers develop a train-as-you're-going-to-fight mentality. The men of the 160th fully understand that they will participate in combat missions.

The 160th SOAR(A) battalions are organized to address the operational needs of the special operations units they support, according to the expected theater of operations, type of mission, and level of conflict. The 160th possesses a variety of capable aircraft, including MH-60 Black Hawk medium-utility helicopters, MH-47 Chinook heavy helicopters, and A/MH-6 Little Bird special operations helicopters.

The AH-6 and MH-6 Little Bird helicopters are direct descendents of the OH-6A Cayuse light observation helicopters used during the Vietnam War. The AH-6 is an attack version used for close aerial support of ground troops and direct action. The MH-6 is a utility aircraft used to insert or extract small combat teams. Little Birds are capable of hot-weather, high-altitude flight. They boast the lowest maintenance-to-flight-hour ratio in the special operations aviation fleet. They can be configured to carry an extensive armament for a specific mission and are equipped with a forward-looking infrared (FLIR) sensor. The helicopter's pilots have a choice of five

Rangers from 3rd Ranger Battalion are stacked at the start and decked out with loads of technologically advanced equipment. Safety is required, and Rangers wear hearing protection, eye protection, and helmets. Each Ranger wears an on-the-move hydration system, or CamelBak, to promote hydration without stopping the exercise. Rangers physically push themselves to the limit every training day.

secure radio networks, including one satellite communications (SATCOM) network to communicate with one another, ground troops, or commanders aboard naval ships.

The AH-6 holds a crew of two without passengers, but boasts an armament of 70mm rocket launchers, M134 7.62mm miniguns, MK19 40mm grenade launchers, air-to-air Stingers, and Hellfire laser-guided missiles. The miniguns are capable of firing 33 rounds per second. The AH-6 can cruise at speeds of 260 kilometers per hour.

The MH-6's principal task is transporting special operations forces into tight situations. The troops ride on two planks attached to the aircraft's sides, enabling the men to disembark immediately upon reaching their destination. The MH-6 Little Bird has a maximum speed of 280 kilometers per hour.

Friends and colleagues greet the winners—Staff Sergeant Adam Nash and Staff Sergeant Colin Boley from the 75th Ranger Regiment—after the two-day best ranger competition's last event. These Rangers competed the entire first day, conducted land navigation during the night, and then competed some more. They continually sustained and encouraged one another, because no one can do it alone.

To provide air support as mobile as the special operations force, the AH-6J special attack aircraft was developed. The AH-6J fits aboard a C-130 cargo plane and can be unpacked and ready to fly five minutes after arrival. Armament includes 2.75-inch rocket pods and Gatling-type 7.62mm miniguns.

The mission-enhanced Little Bird (MELB) program upgraded the rotors, engine, and transmission systems, and improved the structure of the AH-6 and MH-6. These Little Birds have been deployed in Grenada, Panama, the Persian Gulf, Desert Storm, Somalia, and other places, including some that are classified direct actions.

The Sikorsky-made MH-60A Black Hawk has evolved into three variants: the MH-60G, known as the Pave Hawk and used by the U.S. Air Force special operations wings; and the MH-60L and MH-60K, both of which are utilized by the 160th SOAR(A). The Black Hawk variants were among the first to be equipped with the forward-looking infrared (FLIR) sensors, disco light infrared jammer, global positioning system (GPS), auxiliary fuel tanks, infrared suppressive exhausts, SATCOM, radar warning receivers, 7.62mm miniguns, and other cutting-edge special operations technological features. The MH-60-series helicopters can operate from a fixed land facility, remote land site, or ship.

The MH-60L boasts aerial refueling capability, electronics such as color Doppler weather radar, Kevlar ballistic armor, and the capability to carry Hellfire missiles. A new folding tail was added to simplify use aboard naval ships.

The MH-60K is the high-end special operations helicopter saturated with advanced avionics. It features a fully integrated glass cockpit with custom-designed liquid-crystal displays for easier use with night-vision goggles (NVG). The MH-60K flight deck is designed for flying fast and low at night and in nearly zero-visibility weather. It has terrain-following radar, and a FLIR sensor provides complete weather information with map-of-the-earth information to enhance pinpoint navigation despite adverse conditions.

A laser rangefinder allows the crew to detect, identify, and engage targets at an extended range with laser-guided missiles. These Hellfire rockets are mounted on either side of the craft's body on detachable "wings." The direct-action penetrator (DAP) Black Hawk provides armed escorts and fire support.

Accordingly, this variant is equipped with integrated fire control systems and pilot heads-up display (HUD) for highly accurate and effective firepower. The night stalkers designed the DAP version with possible weapons configurations of two 19-round 70mm rocket pods, two 7.62mm miniguns, two forward-firing 30mm chain guns, Hellfire rockets, and Stinger missiles.

An external hydraulic hoist system can lift 600 pounds with up to 200 feet of cable for rescue operations. Mounted on the helicopter's underside, a cargo hook is capable of supporting an external load of 9,000 pounds. Fast rope insertion/extraction systems (FRIES) mounted on either side of the aircraft's body can support 1,500 pounds each. The DAP Black Hawk can carry 12 to 15 Rangers and their equipment over 750 miles without refueling.

Chapter 5

GULF WAR ONE/ WAR ON TERROR

At Malvesti Field in Fort Benning, students low crawl though the muddy water during the seemingly endless physical training. To clear the barbed wire's sharp spurs, students must submerge or carefully turn their heads to the side. The mud gets its red-orange color from the indigenous red Georgia clay. Ranger students are placed in uncomfortable training conditions to push their physical and mental limits to prepare them for the reality of combat where there are no creature comforts.

The Department of Defense has allocated an expansion of the special operations community by adding over 3,900 personnel over fiscal years 2004 to 2009, which will provide the manpower needed to wage a global war on terrorism. The individual special operations forces soldier remains the key element to success in special operations missions worldwide. The needs of the combat-mission Ranger and solutions to these needs are ever-changing, as today's technology is rapidly replaced with more innovative, creative, and successful options. The ranger regiment is equipped with advanced technologies to access, identify, and neutralize all types of conventional explosives, ordnance, and improvised explosive devices (IED), an ominous threat in both Afghanistan and Iraq. Ranger missions benefit from the technologies used to collect timely intelligence and to disseminate crucial intelligence, information, and communication in denied-access areas or hostile situations.

The individual infantry soldier is the central component to any offensive or defensive military action. The soldiers on the ground win wars. The U.S. Army has embraced the concept of the individual soldier as the military's most important weapon system. The ranger battalion is outfitted with its own support element, transportation, and weaponry according to the specialized operational requirements of each mission. The elite and highly skilled individual Ranger is also outfitted with specialized ballistic protection, technology, clothing, and equipment to provide optimal fighting capabilities in any environment and under any condition.

The greatest weapon in the global war on terrorism is still the volunteer American soldier who is highly disciplined, intrinsically motivated,

specifically trained, and proudly wearing the scroll of the 75th Ranger Regiment, whether of the 1st, 2nd, or 3rd battalions. This elite American infantryman will accomplish and complete the mission in spite of insurmountable odds when all other units have declined or failed. He willingly embraces unexpected circumstances in a varied and complicated distant battlefield.

With magazines placed on the front of the ranger body armor (RBA), Rangers find it easier to access ammunition and maintain a greater range of motion. The pouches and pockets are removable and interchangeable according to the operator's preferences. All armored protective vests, RBA, and Rhodesian assault vests have hands-free hydration systems designed into the back for drinking water. Rangers no longer use canteens.

Fast roping is a great way to put lots of Rangers into a small area. It also decreases the risk to the air platform the Rangers operate from by eliminating the time the aircraft would stay on the ground for soldiers to disembark. Rangers can fast rope onto the ground, a roof top, a tight area, or into the water.

Ranger training is continuous, with a more extensive training calendar than any other army unit. With the global war on terrorism overseas, the three ranger battalions in the regiment each rotate to the Middle East. One is in Iraq, another is in Afghanistan, while the final battalion outfits new men and takes care of personal matters at home. Many ranger missions in the global war on terrorism are classified and undisclosed at this time.

Tired, wet, and hungry Rangers on a road march from one training area to another maintain a regular interval of space between themselves. These Rangers from 3rd Ranger Battalion just finished a stress fire, which was an obstacle course and live-fire range integrated into one large exercise. Despite their exhaustion, quit is not in a Ranger's vocabulary.

With the most advanced equipment in the world bestowed upon him and the expectation of success from the world watching, failure is not an option for the Ranger. A grateful nation asks for extraordinary things under extraordinary conditions, and the Ranger quietly and professionally answers.

The brotherhood of these exceptional warriors is bound by their unique experiences on combat missions throughout Central America, Eastern Europe, Africa, and the Middle East. Rangers readily accept missions and travel to distant places in the blink of an eye.

The First Gulf War

When Saddam Hussein invaded Kuwait in 1990, the U.S. response was widely covered in the media. Smart bombs were the

As Rangers prepare to complete their objective, medics and headquarters personnel ready the wounded for extraction and medical transport. This medic pulls a wounded Ranger on a Skedko stretcher. The platoon sergeant and first sergeant position themselves at the tail end of the helicopter's ramp to account for each and every Ranger. No one is left behind.

main focus, and the American public was led to believe that a country could win a war from the air. Although their actions were unpublicized, special operations forces were already deep behind enemy lines. U.S. Navy SEALs executed reconnaissance missions. Army special forces worked with local resistance fighters. Delta Force and the British Secret Air Service (SAS) roamed deep

behind enemy lines, destroying SCUD missiles.

The Rangers fought in Operation Desert Storm. Elements of B Company, 1st Battalion, and one platoon with weapons platoon attachments of A Company, 1st Battalion, deployed to Saudi Arabia from February 12 to April 15, 1991, in support of Operation Desert Storm. The Rangers conducted raids and

A Ranger reviews his responsibilities and actions as he takes an objective with his squad. The squad listens intently so mistakes and poor practices will not be repeated. The squad then has the opportunity to attack the position again. An after-action review (AAR) can take as long as an hour. The practical application of skills in training exercises coupled with immediate feedback and correction in the AAR format drastically enhances new skills.

provided a quick-reaction force in cooperation with Allied forces. They patrolled behind enemy lines in vehicles and on off-road motorcycles. A company-sized element of Rangers attacked an Iraqi radio broadcasting station near the Jordanian border. The Rangers were inserted by Pave Low helicopters and moved to their target. The Rangers rapidly descended on the radio station, seized the objective, and took Iraqis as prisoners and interrogated them. Rangers gathered up or destroyed equipment and documents. When the operation was complete, the Rangers quietly slipped away and disappeared into the darkness.

In December 1991, 1st Battalion and the Regimental Headquarters Company deployed to Kuwait in a routine training exercise as a show of force. The Rangers jumped into Kuwait during daylight hours. D Company, 4th Ranger Training Battalion, sent a squad of ranger instructors to help train soldiers in long-range reconnaissance.

Continuing Operations

Deployments for the 75th Ranger Regiment are ongoing because their expert skill, lightning speed, and commitment to duty are needed to fight the global war on terrorism, particularly in Iraq and Afghanistan. The 75th Ranger Regiment is conducting classified missions during Operation Enduring Freedom (OEF) and Operation Iraqi Freedom (OIF). But due

While practicing for the expert infantryman's badge (EIB), a Ranger at the camouflage station takes full advantage of the local forest's leaves and tree branches and places them on his uniform. This kind of camouflage would most likely be best suited for an ambush where men would lie in wait for the enemy to enter the kill zone. Local vegetation allows seamless concealment from the enemy forces, resulting in the Ranger's trademark element of surprise.

Running to rejoin his squad on a desert mobility vehicle (DMV), a team leader from 3rd Ranger Battalion has all men lock and clear weapons before moving down the road off the live-fire range area. The DMV is the special forces' version of the high-mobility multipurpose wheeled vehicle (HMMWV, or Humvee), tailored for long patrols in the desert environment. The DMV is also known as the ground mobility vehicle (GMV). The early GMV was a modified HMMWV with additional machine gun mounts and the team's radios, weapons, and enough fuel and supplies to operate in the desert for 10 days.

to operational security related to tactics, techniques, and procedures, it may be years before official documents are released to tell the Rangers' stories of Iraq and Afghanistan.

Generally, ranger missions are not openly identified in the media. Instead, reporters indicate the presence of special operations forces, which may or may not include Rangers, SEALs, and other specifically and highly trained soldiers. Areas of operations for the 75th Ranger Regiment are usually identified when a Ranger's death is made public.

Rangers have bravely seized airfields in western Iraq and raided enemy strongholds. They retained control of the Haditha Dam on the Euphrates River, keeping Saddam

Soldiers from A Company, 1st Ranger Battalion, 75th Ranger Regiment, deployed to Fort Campbell, Kentucky, participate in live-fire training August 31, 2004.
Gillian M. Albro, USASOC PAO

Hussein's men from destroying it. They have willingly fought in the caves of Tora Bora, the mountains of Afghanistan, and the rugged desert of Iraq.

Operation Rhino-Afghanistan

The operation began the night of October 19–20, 2001, and was over before the sun rose. This action marked the first major ground operation in Afghanistan. The Rangers' mission was to gather intelligence about the location of the Taliban and al Qaeda leadership.

During Operation Rhino, at least 100 3rd Battalion Rangers silently parachuted out of the night sky onto an airstrip at Bibi Tera in Helmand province, 80 miles southwest of the Taliban stronghold at Kandahar. It was suspected that the airfield was used for drug and gun running. The Rangers landed, split up into their individual weapons teams, and

moved quickly to secure the area. The Rangers stayed on the ground for two to three hours. Intelligence was gathered regarding the possible future use of the airstrip. Iraqis were interrogated, numerous weapons and ammunition were captured, and the operation left more than 20 Taliban fighters dead. Still covered by darkness, the withdrawal began and the Rangers' helicopters returned them to a Pakistani border airstrip. On November 25, 2001, U.S. Marines occupied the site of the ranger assault and designated their new airstrip facility Camp Rhino.

Although each helicopter that flew to Afghanistan returned unharmed, there were American casualties—the first in the war. Specialist John J. Edmunds and Specialist Kristofor Stonesifer, both of 3rd Battalion, 75th Ranger Regiment, were killed in a Black Hawk helicopter crash upon the return of the extraction mission. The crash occurred at the Pakistan airstrip.

A mass tactical jump is the beginning of the mission. Those with crew-served weapon systems are the first to exit the aircraft, since the weapons produce the most casualties in the event that the aircraft takes on fire and the remaining jumpers must unexpectedly cease exiting.

Jumping with a small assault pack, a Ranger from 1st Ranger Battalion de-rigs his equipment. Waiting inside the aircraft to jump can be a very loud and trying experience, but after you exit the door, hit the prop blast, and withstand the opening shock of your parachute, it's like the world is free of noise. The calm and quiet is truly spiritual . . . as long as no one is firing at you.

For a second group of Rangers and Delta Force commandos, the target was Baba Sahib, a village of mud huts with straw roofs about five miles from the Taliban capital of Kandahar. Surrounded by mountains, the Afghan's stronghold of Baba Sahib never fell to the Russians during the 1980s. It was a different story when the Rangers descended in a single, swift attack. Rangers slid down fast ropes from helicopters into the compound. Baba Sahib had a small garrison to guard the home of a Taliban leader, Mullah Omar, whose home was made of brick and concrete. The village holds a special place in the psyche of the Afghans. Rangers were engaged in a heated firefight, but were extracted to safety. Omar was nowhere to be found.

With a rush of wind and adrenaline, the Rangers glide down through the overcast skies. The airborne Ranger must look out for the other jumpers and check his rate of descent. He checks his canopy, and uses the risers and toggles to control the chute before implementing his landing technique.

Rangers train for nuclear, biological, and chemical (NBC) attacks. This Ranger wears an M40 protective mask and holds an anti-nerve agent injection, pralidoxine chloride. If the Ranger comes in contact with a nerve agent, this injection will diminish the effects.

Muddy, wet Rangers line up to participate in more physical training. Rangers will modify their physical training activities by creating unusual and innovative ways of working out. Terrain runs, which the company commander will lead, can go through creeks, over dumpsters, and through parking lots. It keeps the training challenging for the Rangers, with an added bit of fun.

Operation Anaconda and Operation Mountain Resolve-Afghanistan

The 1st Ranger Battalion was called to action in 2002 for Operation Anaconda with the mission to secure Takur Ghar, a 10,000-foot snow-capped mountain in eastern Afghanistan, as an observation post for the nearby valleys. The al Qaeda enemy had a well-concealed, fortified stronghold within the crooks, crannies, and shadows of the Shahikot mountains, with artillery positioned to shoot down aircraft flying in the valley below. On March 4, 2002, Rangers implemented Task Force Mountain against the al Qaeda terrorists. The Rangers experienced problems as the terrain hampered their line-of-sight communications. The intense 17-hour firefight atop a frigid, rugged mountain ridge with sheer drop-offs ended with the Rangers and accompanying forces securing the mountain top, the deaths of approximately 450 Taliban and al Qaeda soldiers defending the mountain, and the

deaths of three Rangers of the 1st Battalion.

Signals between Ranger, special operations force, and Task Force 160 global positioning system (GPS) navigational equipment and satellites in space may be blocked by the 10,000-foot-or-higher surrounding mountains of Afghanistan. For this reason, the Rangers continue to train with an altimeter, which measures height, as a backup to GPS. The altimeter is preferred to the compass, because the compass requires dead reckoning and counting paces.

In the rugged mountains of Hindu Kush in northeastern Afghanistan, helicopter pilots experienced brown-outs when landing in the deserts. The 160th Special Operations Aviation Regiment's pilots called it rotor borealis, the light show put on by sand friction against the rotor blades. Unfortunately, rotor blades stirring up dust and debris while landing caused a search-and-rescue helicopter to crash in Pakistan, killing two U.S. crew

"Getting smoked" for no reason is just part of ranger school. It can happen anywhere: waiting in the chow line, signing out weapons from the arms room, going to church on Sunday. Even if you are the most squared away individual, a ranger instructor will have something for you when you least expect it. Come to ranger school in shape and ready to push away on that red Georgia clay.

members. The helicopter was supporting a mission for a special forces raid near Kandahar.

On the weekend of November 7–9, 2003, the United States began a large-scale assault in Afghanistan's northeast provinces of Kunar and Nuristan. Named Operation Mountain Resolve, the focus in the mountainous Hindu Kush area was the result of increased insurgent activity. Men of the 2nd Battalion, 75th Ranger Regiment, conducted combat patrols as part of Operation Mountain Resolve. On such a patrol in the Kunar province, Sergeant Jay A. Blessing was killed on November 14, 2003, when an improvised explosive device exploded in the vicinity of his convoy. Coalition officials characterized the explosion as a hostile attack by enemy anti-coalition forces.

For months, U.S. special operations forces had been searching for Taliban and al Qaeda leaders who were believed to be hiding in Afghanistan's mountainous terrain near the Pakistan border. Ranger platoons moved from one assignment to the next, scouring the area and taking part in sporadic skirmishes and firefights.

Members of the 1st Ranger Battalion come together to receive medals for bravery while conducting the rescue of prisoner of war Private Jessica Lynch from Iraq. The 1st Ranger Battalion had the primary mission to enter the hospital and retrieve Private Lynch from the enemy.

Rangers patrol their designated area in central Iraq in a ground mobility vehicle (GMV). The gunner posted on top of the vehicle uses an M2 Browning .50-caliber machine gun for security as the patrol performs its mission. Two Rangers face the GMV's rear and two more face to each side with weapons ready. Although these vehicles traverse the desert land well, they lack the much-needed armor for protection.

A ranger squad is poised outside the door seconds prior to breaching the door and clearing the room of enemy personnel. The practice of clearing rooms is rehearsed repeatedly with each member of the squad assigned specific tasks. The end result is a procedure that runs like clockwork and a room devoid of enemy personnel.

On April 22, 2004, the platoon of 2nd Battalion Rangers moved a combat patrol through the mountainous terrain about 90 miles south of Kabul and 25 miles southwest of a military base in Khowst, Afghanistan. While heading past the village of Sperah, one of the platoon's vehicles became inoperable and irreparable. Airlift for the disabled vehicle was not available, and the soldiers towed the vehicle instead of abandoning it. The platoon split, sending a working vehicle ahead while the remaining Rangers towed the disabled one.

Approximately 30 minutes after the platoon split, the Rangers hampered by the disabled vehicle were suddenly ambushed with small-arms and mortar fire by anti-coalition forces. Rangers, including Specialist Patrick Tillman, exited the vehicle and engaged in an intense firefight with a dozen enemy fighters shooting from multiple locations. It was dusk, and light conditions were poor. Upon hearing the engagement, the other section of the platoon rapidly returned to the location of the ambush and engaged in the fight. An Afghan fighter was mistaken for the enemy by a ranger squad leader, who shot the Afghan soldier. The other

Rangers observed the direction of fire by the squad leader and oriented their fire in the same direction. Tillman, standing beside the Afghan soldier, was also shot. Two other Rangers were injured by friendly fire. Specialist Tillman bravely responded to enemy fire and shot at the enemy during a 20-minute firefight before he was killed.

Nassiriya and Hadithah Dam—Iraq

Private Jessica Lynch, a 19-year-old army supply clerk, was a member of the U.S. Army's 507th Ordnance Maintenance Company. Her convoy took a wrong turn near Nassiriya and was ambushed, and nine of Lynch's comrades were killed. Iraqi soldiers took Lynch to the local hospital, which reportedly was inundated with Fedayeen, black-clad Iraqi security agents. Lynch was held for eight days. Mohammed Al Rehaief, an Iraqi lawyer, realized she was at the hospital and informed U.S. troops. He also supplied information about the number of troops and made hand-drawn maps of the building's layout. Just after midnight on April 1, 2003, 1st Battalion Rangers and U.S. Navy SEALs stormed the Nassiriya hospital and rescued Lynch in a swift nighttime raid.

Rangers Killed in Action in the Global War on Terrorism

Specialist John J. Edmunds
3rd Ranger Battalion, 75th Ranger Regiment
Operation Enduring Freedom
Killed in action, October 19, 2001

Specialist Kristofor T. Stonesifer
3rd Ranger Battalion, 75th Ranger Regiment
Operation Enduring Freedom
Killed in action, October 19, 2001

Specialist Marc A. Anderson
1st Ranger Battalion, 75th Ranger Regiment
Operation Enduring Freedom
Killed in action, March 4, 2002

Corporal Matthew A. Commons
1st Ranger Battalion, 75th Ranger Regiment
Operation Enduring Freedom
Killed in action, March 4, 2002

Sergeant Bradley S. Crose
1st Ranger Battalion, 75th Ranger Regiment
Operation Enduring Freedom
Killed in action, March 4, 2002

Staff Sergeant Nino D. Livaudais
3rd Ranger Battalion, 75th Ranger Regiment
Operation Iraqi Freedom
Killed in action, April 3, 2003

Specialist Ryan P. Long
3rd Ranger Battalion, 75th Ranger Regiment
Operation Iraqi Freedom
Killed in action, April 3, 2003

Captain Russell B. Rippetoe
3rd Ranger Battalion, 75th Ranger Regiment
Operation Iraqi Freedom
Killed in action, April 3, 2003

Corporal Andrew F. Chris
3rd Ranger Battalion, 75th Ranger Regiment
Operation Iraqi Freedom
Killed in action, June 26, 2003

Sergeant Timothy M. Conneway
3rd Ranger Battalion, 75th Ranger Regiment
Operation Iraqi Freedom
Killed in action, June 28, 2003

Sergeant Jay A. Blessing
2nd Ranger Battalion, 75th Ranger Regiment
Operation Enduring Freedom
Killed in action, November 14, 2003

Specialist Patrick D. Tillman
2nd Ranger Battalion, 75th Ranger Regiment
Operation Enduring Freedom
Killed in action, April 22, 2004

Private First Class Nathan E. Stahl
2nd Ranger Battalion, 75th Ranger Regiment
Operation Iraqi Freedom
Killed in action, September 21, 2004

Corporal William M. Amundson
3rd Ranger Battalion, 75th Ranger Regiment
Operation Enduring Freedom
Killed in action, October 18, 2004

The U.S. Army Rangers' initial seizure of the Hadithah Dam occurred the night of April 1, 2003. The dam is located on the Euphrates River, 125 miles northwest of Karbala, Iraq. Seizure of the Hadithah Dam and hydropower facility prevented its possible destruction by Iraqi forces. Destruction of this critical structure would result in a non-traditional weapon of mass destruction, as release of its water would cause extensive flooding, loss of electrical power, and lack of water supply for the Iraqi people during the summer months. That night, the Rangers engaged in a heated firefight and responded to repeated attacks against their hold on the dam. Artillery and mortars were shot by counter special operations units operating from the town of Hadithah. Rangers of B Company, 3rd Ranger Battalion, with elements of the 1st Ranger Battalion, fought for nearly three weeks against a determined Iraqi enemy to retain their control of the Hadithah Dam. Rangers

On March 3, 2002, three Rangers from 1st Ranger Battalion were killed fighting the Taliban and al Qaeda enemy in Afghanistan during Operation Anaconda. Sergeant Bradley S. Crose, Specialist Marc A. Anderson, and Corporal Matthew A. Commons paid the ultimate sacrifice for their country. Members of the firing squad ready for a 21-gun salute.

supported joint special operations task force—west from April 2–24, 2003, until the 4th Infantry Division assumed responsibility for the area.

Elements of the 3rd Ranger Battalion parachuted into Iraq to secure a checkpoint approximately 11 miles southwest of the Hadithah Dam. At this checkpoint, late in the day on April 3, 2003, a civilian sport utility vehicle approached the military checkpoint, and a pregnant Iraqi woman jumped out of the vehicle, ran toward the Rangers, and screamed in fear. The vehicle exploded, possibly detonated by the man inside. The blast killed the pregnant Iraqi woman, a man and a woman inside the vehicle, and three Rangers of the 3rd Battalion— Captain Russell Rippetoe, Staff Sergeant Nino Livaudais, and Specialist Ryan Long. Two other 3rd Battalion Rangers, Specialist Chad Thibodeau and Specialist Kyle Smith, were wounded. U.S. Brigadier General Vincent Brooks characterized the bombing as a terrorist action.

A conventional tank unit arrived at the Tallil Airfield in Iraq early on April 2, 2004. The tank unit linked up with special operations forces and transported 10 M1A1 tanks, three M113 armored personnel carriers, an FST-V fire-support vehicle, two fuel trucks, three cargo trucks, and a Humvee by C-17 aircraft to H-1 Airfield in western Iraq. On arrival at H-1 Airfield, the tank company came under the control of the 1st Battalion, 75th Ranger Regiment. The Rangers and the tank company road marched 160 kilometers east. On May 22, 2004, another conventional forces company road marched to Tallil Airbase and then airlifted to another airbase in western Iraq. There, the units were attached to the 3rd Ranger Battalion. Reorganization of tasks and integration of conventional and special operations forces units demonstrate the unstoppable power of their joint efforts to meet the ever-changing tactical and operational situation in the global war on terrorism.

The Ranger Creed

Recognizing that I volunteered as a Ranger, fully knowing the hazards of my chosen profession, I will always endeavor to uphold the prestige, honor, and high esprit de corps of my ranger regiment.

Acknowledging the fact that a Ranger is a more elite soldier who arrives at the cutting edge of battle by land, sea, or air, I accept the fact that as a Ranger my country expects me to move further, faster, and fight harder than any other soldier.

Never shall I fail my comrades, I will always keep myself mentally alert, physically strong, and morally straight, and I will shoulder more than my share of the task whatever it may be, one hundred percent and then some.

Gallantly will I show the world that I am a specially selected and well trained soldier. My courtesy to superior officers, neatness of dress, and care of equipment shall set the example for others to follow.

Energetically will I meet the enemies of my country. I shall defeat them on the field of battle for I am better trained and will fight with all my might. Surrender is not a ranger word. I will never leave a fallen comrade to fall into the hands of the enemy and under no circumstances will I ever embarrass my country.

Readily will I display the intestinal fortitude required to fight on to the ranger objective and complete the mission, though I be the lone survivor.

Rangers lead the way!

At the Cathedral of Saint John the Baptist in Savannah, Georgia, home of the 1st Ranger Battalion, roses spill forth and across the floor. The battalion respectfully gathers to honor the memory of three fallen comrades lost in Afghanistan fighting the Taliban and al Qaeda.

"Recognizing that I volunteered as a Ranger, fully knowing the hazards of my chosen profession, I will always endeavor to uphold the prestige, honor, and high esprit de corps of my ranger regiment." A helmet with dog tags and weapon of a Ranger killed in Operation Anaconda, Afghanistan, in March 2002.

"I believe the ranger regiment's greatest success over the past year has been the ability to transition from sustained combat operations in Afghanistan back to decisive combat operations in Iraq, back to sustained combat operations in both Afghanistan and Iraq, without a period of recovery," said Colonel James Nixon, ranger regimental commander. "Over the last year, the ranger regiment has conducted combat operations with almost every deployed special operations force, conventional, and coalition force in both Afghanistan and Iraq. It has also continued to recruit, assess, and train the next generation of Rangers and ranger leadership." Over 70 percent of the U.S. Army Rangers have conducted multiple combat deployments, and many are on their fifth or sixth rotations since 9/11.